BEING GOOD

BEING

BUDDHIST ETHICS FOR EVERYDAY LIFE

GOOD

By Master Hsing Yun
translated by Tom Graham

New York • **WEATHERHILL** • *Tokyo*

First edition, 1998

Published by Weatherhill, Inc.
568 Broadway, Suite 705
New York, NY 10012

Library of Congress Cataloging-in-Publication Data

Hsing, Yün.
    Being good: Buddhist ethics for everyday life / Yun Hsing; translated by Tom
Graham.
        p.   cm.
    ISBN 0-8348-0458-1
    1. Religious life—Buddhism.   2. Buddhism—Doctrines.   I. Graham, Tom
(Thomas Boyd), 1951–   . II. Title
BQ4302.H75 1998
294.3'5—dc21   98-37910
                                                                            CIP

Contents

Foreword

I am delighted to have been asked to write this brief introduction to Master Hsing Yun's newest publication, *Being Good*. This masterly presentation of the most pragmatic aspects of Buddhist ethics in action is the culmination of many years of scholarship and deep reflection. The erudition of the author is established most convincingly by the citations he has chosen and by his explanations of them.

No aspect of life is omitted. Master Hsing Yun has demonstrated that the deep-rooted pragmatism of Buddhism makes it a religion valid today and for all times. In addition to this, he shows us how to apply the teachings of the Buddha to our daily lives.

In *Being Good*, Master Hsing Yun displays his unwavering faith in the universality of Buddhism. Neither in the teachings recounted nor in the texts cited does he show any partiality to a particular tradition of Buddhism. It is only natural that he should cite many Mahayana sources, especially when they comprise the bulk of the Chinese tradition, but his desire to achieve a comprehensiveness of treatment makes him delve into the Dhammapada, the Sigalovada Sutta and several other sources which are more often associated with the Theravadan tradition.

Master Hsing Yun frequently uses quotes from the historical Buddha, whatever be the source that has preserved his wisdom. In doing so, he has set a worthy example for scholars who could enrich their discussions on various aspects of Buddhism if only they had an equally open mind on the unity which supersedes the diversity of Buddhism.

The translation of *Being Good* is presented in a distinctly lucid, absorbing, and readable style. These essays can be read with unabated interest. As a translator of Pali and Sanskrit I am able to appreciate how well the translator has been able to render Master Hsing Yun's wise teachings in the plainest and most beautiful language.

This book is a great gift to readers of English all over the world. In *Being Good*, Master Hsing Yun has made it easier and pleasanter for all of us to deepen our understanding of the wisdom of Buddhism.

Ananda W. P. Guruge

Former Ambassador of Sri Lanka
to the United States

Translator's Preface

Though he is virtually unknown in the West, Master Hsing Yun is probably the most famous Chinese monk alive today. He is renowned for his speaking ability and for his kindness. These qualities have helped him bring the wisdom of Buddhism to literally hundreds of thousands of people in Taiwan, Hong Kong, and throughout the world.

The essays that make up *Being Good* originally were part of a longer work on humanistic Buddhism by Master Hsing Yun. In 1997, he asked me to translate them into English. I was more than happy to do so because I felt that these essays were excellent representations of the energy and compassion that have moved Master Hsing Yun to preach the Dharma for almost sixty years. In *Being Good*, Master Hsing Yun shows us how to apply the wisdom of Buddhism to life in this world. He shows us how to control anger, how to deal with loss and suffering, and how to increase our well-being by living lives that are in perfect accord with the precepts of Buddhism.

I hope that this volume will, in some small way, serve as an introduction to the work of Master Hsing Yun. His compassionate dedication to the well-being of others is an example all of us can follow, whether we have chosen the monastic path or not.

In closing, I want to thank Master Hsing Yun and the members of Buddha's Light International Association for their continued support and encouragement for these translations.

May any and all merit that may accrue from this work be shared by sentient beings everywhere.

Tom Graham

BEING GOOD

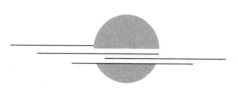

The Eight Winds

Profit and loss, defamation and fame,
praise and blame, suffering and joy;
all of these are impermanent and thus
why should any of them cause satisfaction
or dissatisfaction?

— from the *Mahasanghika Vinaya*

The Eight Winds are the eight conditions mentioned in the first two lines of the verse above. The Buddha taught that these eight conditions are a natural part of life. All of us will experience each of these states many times in many lives. The Buddha also taught that we should not allow ourselves to be blown off course by any of the Eight Winds. Instead, we should regard them as temporary conditions that present us with a chance to learn something new. As long as we feel unduly concerned about any of them, we can be sure we still have something to learn.

If we do not stop and think deeply about all of the Eight Winds, we will tend to believe that profit, fame, praise, and joy are better than loss, defamation, blame, and suffering. This tendency is a very good access point that can help us understand to just what degree we believe that the delusion of having a separate self is real.

The highest goal of Buddhism is to become fully enlightened within the perfect wisdom of our inherent Buddha nature. This wisdom completely transcends all delusions of selfhood. This state has been achieved many times by Buddhists in the past and there is no reason why it cannot be achieved by many of us who are alive today. Contemplating the impermanence and essential sameness of all of the Eight Winds is a very good method for helping us see beyond the delusions of the self-centered self.

The "joy" mentioned among the Eight Winds is samsaric joy, the transitory joy of the phenomenal world, not the joy that is a natural part of the enlightened mind. Think about the Eight Winds: is fame really so wonderful? Is profit all we want from life? Is praise always good for us? Deep analysis of any loss will always bring us to a higher level of wisdom. Would we really be stimulated to contemplate life's inherent transience if everything went the way we wanted all the time? The Eight Winds are winds; they come and go. They arise like the weather. Tomorrow will always be different from today.

There is a Chinese text called *Instructions Pertaining to the Royal Samadhi of Contemplating the Buddha*. This text contains excellent advice on how to remain even-minded and balanced no matter which wind is blowing today. It teaches us to look deeply into our circumstances so that we will be able to derive the greatest benefit from them. This work contains the following ten points:

1) Concerning the body: do not ask to be free of all illness, for when the body is free of all illness, greed quickly arises. When greed has arisen, the precepts soon are broken and progress becomes regression.

2) Concerning the management of worldly affairs: do not ask that any chore be an easy one, for when things go too easily, pride is soon born in the mind. When pride is born in the mind, one soon becomes flippant and deceitful.

3) Concerning thought: do not ask that thinking always be without obstruction, for when thinking is without obstruction, it quickly becomes feverish and irregular. When thinking becomes feverish and irregular, one soon will become deluded and believe that the false is true and the true is false.

4) Concerning the practice of Buddhism: do not ask that there be no trials, for when one is never tried, one's vows will not be strong.

When one's vows are not strong, one can easily be led into believing that one has achieved what one has not achieved.

5) Concerning the making of plans: do not ask that they always be easily made, for when plans are always easy to make, one's will becomes weak and ineffectual. When the will is weak and ineffectual, one is easily led to believe that one's abilities are less than they are.

6) Concerning friendship: do not ask that matters always go your way for when one always gets one's own way, one soon will lose a sense of right and wrong. When one loses a sense of right and wrong, one quickly slides into the tendency to blame others for anything that goes awry.

7) Concerning people: do not ask that others always follow your lead for when others always follow one's lead, one will soon become arrogant. When one has become arrogant, one will begin to grasp tightly onto the attachments of the ego.

8) Concerning morality: do not ask for rewards for moral behavior for if one is always rewarded for moral behavior, one will soon become calculating in everything one does. Once one has become calculating, one will begin to crave fame and a good reputation.

9) Concerning profits: do not always ask to obtain a part of them for when one always gets a part of all profits, one soon will become lazy and dull. Once one has become lazy and dull, one will quickly hurt oneself.

10) Concerning false accusations: do not try to justify yourself or make explanations, for self-justifications only increase the illusion of having a separate self. Once this illusion of a separate self arises, thoughts of anger and revenge soon will follow.

Once we have learned to think in the ways described above, we will be much closer to being able to concentrate on what we are doing and not on what we are getting. The value of this life and of all our future lives is determined by what we are doing now and not by what we are getting now. This point is very important. Everything that happens to us should be perceived as an opportunity for growth.

*All who cultivate themselves in
Mahayana samadhi,
and all who enter upon the
bodhisattva way,
begin with the ordinary and
through that achieve Nirvana.*

— from the *Lankavatara Sutra*

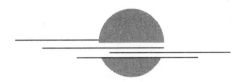

Progress and Morality

Careful in speech, controlled in body,
aware of the workings of the mind;
patient under insult, never angry;
this is the path of great progress.

— from the *Dharmapada*

Careful in speech, controlled in body

In this complex world we must know how to behave if we want to make progress. The world contains so many kinds of people and so many different levels of morality and wisdom, we must have some basic guidelines which can fit all situations. Being careful about what we say while controlling the urges of the body is a very good basic guideline for all situations.

Control of the body means that we know when to act and when not to act, and that we know how to behave with moderation. If we see something that contradicts our understanding of the Dharma, it is usually best to ignore it because, in the first place, we might be wrong about what we think, and in the second place, we should always remember that every person must learn in his own way. When we do decide to speak or act, we should always be as compassionate as we are able. Compassion itself is a guide that always prompts us to be tolerant, patient, and as wise as possible.

It is very important to be careful about speech. This is especially true nowadays since so many different cultures and groups are presently intermingling with each other. What is inoffensive in your group may be very offensive in someone else's. What is a joke to you may be a rebuke or an insult to someone else. The vast and ever-changing variety of the world does not allow us to stop at every moment and fully explain exactly what we meant and why we said it. In an ideal world, people would all understand each other perfectly. However, in this world misunderstandings are very common. For this reason, it is very important to be careful about what you say.

There is a Chinese folk saying that goes, "A good word melts the cold of March, while a bad word can freeze the month of June." A single word can save a nation or it can ruin it. We can cause great harm with our words, but we can also bring about great good through them.

In our practice of Buddhism, we should constantly be trying to bring positive energy into whatever situation we find ourselves in. Words are one of the best means we have to facilitate this process. Words should be used to encourage and help other people. They should be used to communicate deeply and warmly. And they should be used to spread the truth of the Dharma to all who will listen.

The Buddha taught that none of us should ever use words to lie, flatter, be harsh, or mislead. In the end, all acts of body and speech should be directed toward the greater welfare of all sentient beings. One can make samsaric gains through body and speech, but as the Buddha said:

> Ananda, all the people in heaven
> only got there through ordinary decency;
> when their good karma is used up,
> they will re-enter the cycle of birth and death.
> In contrast, the bodhisattva makes steady
> progress through his explorations of samadhi,
> through his transfer of merit and
> through his cultivation of the saintly way
> which leads beyond all birth and death.

> — from the *Shurangama Sutra*

Aware of the workings of the mind

The *Avatamsaka Sutra* says, "The mind controls everything." In order to properly control body and speech, we must come to understand our minds. If we can control our minds, we can do anything. Master Hsing K'ung (780–862) wrote a wonderful passage which expresses this point very well. He said, "The practice of Buddhism can be compared to presiding over a walled city: during the day, thieves and bandits must be kept at bay while at night one must be constantly alert. If the mind in charge is thoughtful and able, then there will be peace without the use of weapons."

In Master Hsing K'ung's metaphor the city is the virtuous mind, while the bandits are the six senses that are constantly trying to steal our peace and wisdom.

We must have many tools in our chest when we decide to truly gain control over our minds. Sometimes we must restrict ourselves quite severely and sometimes we must allow our thoughts to soar on the wings of inspiration. In the end:

> *Once a bodhisattva*
> *is committed to the bodhi mind,*
> *he must not stop.*
> *Once he begins to seek the Mahayana way,*
> *he must not become fatigued*
> *and he must not*
> *become tired of the Dharma*
> *or feel that he is satisfied*
> *with what little he has.*

> — from the *Avatamsaka Sutra*

Patient under insult, never angry

What is an insult but an affront to the false sense of self? And what is anger but an attempt to destroy insults? That is all they are; when the false sense of self feels threatened with a loss of control, it reacts with anger. The Buddha emphasized the importance of being patient under insult many times. In this life, all of us will experience insult and derision. Saints react with equanimity and patience while others react in all their many ways, not one of which does anything to solve the deeper problem.

The *Sutra of Bequeathed Teachings* says, "There is nothing better than patience in the cultivation of virtue, morality and the practice of Buddhism." It also says, "One who knows how to be patient gains great power. If you cannot joyfully quaff the poison of evil insults as if you were quaffing sweet dew, then you cannot yet be called wise."

To be patient and to endure insult does not mean that you must be weak or timid. It means that you productively use even your most negative experiences to grow and learn. If you can learn to endure insult and humiliation, you will become very strong.

The *Fachi Sutra* speaks of six kinds of merit gained by a bodhisattva who learns to be patient under insult:

1) If a bodhisattva can listen to insults as if he were merely listening to an echo in a mountain gorge, then he will have achieved "the wisdom of sound."

2) If a bodhisattva can endure being beaten as if he were merely watching forms move in a mirror, then he will have achieved "the wisdom of forms."

3) If a bodhisattva can endure suffering as if he were merely watching an empty illusion, then he will have achieved "the wisdom of illusion."

4) If a bodhisattva can endure anger, then he will have achieved "the wisdom of inner purity."

5) If a bodhisattva can endure the Eight Winds, then he will have achieved "the wisdom of phenomenal purity."

6) If a bodhisattva is not polluted by the troubles of life, then he will have achieved "the wisdom of manifest conditions."

As Buddhists, we must constantly raise our eyes to the higher realms and always remember that:

> *All troubles, all habits, all continuity*
> *all are devoid of essence, all are empty.*
>
> — from the *Mahaprajnaparamita Sutra*

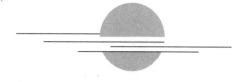

Control of the Body

Now we have a body, a mind, and the Dharma.
No longer is it difficult to teach others.
If you want to teach others, you
must first learn yourself.

— from the *Control of the Body Sutra*

Confucius once said, "If a person has good control over himself, others will follow him without being ordered to do so. If a person has no control over himself, others will not follow him even if ordered to do so."

Karma is generated through body, mouth, and mind. Wise introspection must illuminate each of these three. They must be raised together toward higher awareness and greater self-control. One of the best places to begin getting control of yourself is through your body. The mind is subtle and fickle and more difficult to control than the body. Each of us should strive to achieve basic physical standards for our bodies; we should all try to keep them as fit, as clean,and as well-controlled as possible. We should all strive to gain some measure of control over our basic muscle movements and bodily functions; fidgeting, nail biting, scratching, yawning, and other nervous habits should eventually come under the control of our minds. Exercise, sleep, and eating habits should be reasonable and conducive to physical health and social harmony.

When one takes reasonable care of the body, one will find that the basic precepts of Buddhism are easier to keep. Physical training and self-control need not be over-emphasized. However, basic care and control of the body can be an important starting point for the successful practice of Buddhism.

If one's sleeping habits are as regular and reasonable as possible, one will probably find that many other good habits will fall into line almost of themselves. Laziness, or an unwillingness to participate in life may give way to a more positive and productive attitude once one begins to control one's sleeping habits. Sensuality and self-indulgence may begin to disappear once one begins to get control over one's food intake. The intake of food is closely related to the intake of drugs or alcohol, both of which were proscribed by the Buddha. One's ability to be of service to others may increase once one begins to get regular exercise and sufficient fresh air. The body is only one part of our being, but it is a fundamental and very important part. Without it we would not be able to learn or practice the Dharma.

The body should be controlled in a relaxed and reasonable manner. The following are some basic guidelines that should be considered by all of us:

1) Proper rest. Proper rest is very important. People all have different sleep needs and all of us will have different needs at different times in our lives. Each of us should wisely decide how much sleep is right for us. Some people have a tendency to sleep too much while others have a tendency not to sleep enough. Both of these extremes should be avoided.

2) Proper exercise. All of us should get some exercise every day. A minimum amount for a healthy adult is twenty minutes or more of walking every day; forty or forty-five minutes is optimum. Younger people should engage in more strenuous exercise than walking if they are able.

3) Proper eating. The Buddha taught his followers to be balanced in everything they do, and this certainly includes eating. Since each person is different from all others, each person must decide for himself what the best foods for his body are. Generally, processed foods, processed sugars, and artificial ingredients are not good for human

health, though they can be tolerated in moderation. Meat-eating should be avoided if possible, or at least kept to a minimum. Fresh vegetables and fresh fruits will almost always be beneficial to one's health. Both over-eating and under-eating should be avoided.

The above recommendations are offered as suggestions for minimal maintenance of good health. Once good health has been achieved, it should be treasured and used for learning the Dharma and helping other sentient beings. Good health is not an end in itself, but a means to spiritual growth. The health of our bodies should not become a preoccupation. Vanity about the body or fussiness about what foods may or may not be eaten are sensual indulgences just as much as sloth or gluttony are.

The body should be used to help other sentient beings. The Buddha spoke often of the three aspects of human life—body, mouth, and mind. Normally, all three of these function together. When we focus our attention on the body, however, we can see that the body is the last step in most acts in which the precepts are broken. Killing, stealing, sensual indulgence, lying, and the use of drugs or alcohol are all transgressions committed with our bodies. If our bodies are well-controlled, there is a good chance that we will be able to stop ourselves from breaking the precepts at the last moment, even when our minds have become weak or our mouths have provided us with false rationalizations.

Anyone who practices Buddhism for long will learn that physical and mental control are intimately interrelated. If the mind can be controlled, so can the body. Likewise, if the body can be controlled, so can the mind. Chanting and meditation are two basic Buddhist practices in which mind and body very clearly come together to act as one. Together they pursue the same goal and together they learn that, in truth, there is no separation between them. One cannot exist without the other.

The samadhi states achieved in chanting or in meditation can only be achieved after the body and mind have learned to act in perfect harmony. A fidgeting body cannot achieve samadhi and a dancing mind cannot achieve samadhi. Once both have been controlled, samadhi can be achieved. The basis of all meditation is physical stillness. Wonders can be attained once one has learned simply to sit still. The stillness of perfect concentration or perfect mindfulness is the baseline of all mental functions. Once this stillness has been experienced, the flaring of thoughts and illusions which flame out of it will never appear the same again. The Buddhist understanding of equanimity and emptiness are based on the stillness discovered in deep meditation. Access to this understanding is gained first through control of the body and secondly through control of the mind. Once both have been controlled, samadhi occurs naturally. Once samadhi has been achieved, emptiness and equanimity will be understood.

The *Dharmapada* says, "Victory over a thousand thousand enemies is not as valuable as victory over oneself."

> *Controlled in body, controlled in mind,*
> *seated cross-legged in meditation,*
> *without other thoughts,*
> *focused perfectly on the present,*
> *one contemplates truth with all the mind.*
> *Beyond all greed and attachment,*
> *beyond the defilements of the world,*
> *desire has nowhere to rise.*

— from the *Ekottarika Agama*

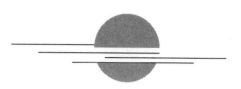

Controlling Speech

Guard against the four verbal transgressions,
Frequently use encouraging speech,
Honestly admit your own mistakes,
and in these ways you will attain
the supreme voice.

— from the *Bodhisattva Without Possessions Sutra*

One word can save a country and one word can destroy a nation. Words are very powerful. Words can be used to bring great harm to others or to bring benefit to them. The mind controls the mouth, but the mouth often seems to be able to talk by itself without forethought or any consideration for the consequences of what it says. The reason for this is language is so close to us—it is such an important part of our minds—that it often becomes animated seemingly without our consent. This is why the Buddha constantly exhorted his followers to watch what they say. It is too easy to say the wrong thing.

The *Sutra Concerning Four Kinds of Self-Harming* says:

In the light of truth, contemplate the tumbling and
roiling of this world; observe that all of it comes from
arguing over unimportant matters. Calamity issues
from the mouth, causing a thousand sins and a myriad
of transgressions which bind us firmly to this realm.

Wise practitioners are careful about what they say and they take the Buddha very seriously when he says to completely avoid the four transgressions of the mouth: lying, duplicity, harsh speech, and idle speech. Nothing good will ever come of them.

The *Sutra on Distinguishing Between the Origins of Good and Evil* says:

> *In this world, no one should harm another through lying, duplicity, harsh speech, or idle speech. If one does not commit these transgressions, one will attain five good results. What are these five results?*
>
> *These results are* 1) *one's words will always be believed,* 2) *one will be loved by others,* 3) *one's breath will be fragrant,* 4) *one will be reborn in heaven and be respected by all,* 5) *when one is reborn again in the human realm, one will get along well with others and others will not be inclined to speak harshly of one.*

Lying

Lying is particularly reprehensible because lying is a deliberate attempt to increase delusion. Most people already are completely lost in delusion; to deliberately add to the problem is to turn away from the bodhisattva way and from the infinite compassion which inspires it. Lying is very damaging because it ruins trust and it causes honest people to doubt their own intuitions. The Buddha called lying one of the ten evil deeds, and he made it the subject of one of his five basic precepts.

The *Chu Fa Chi Yao Sutra* says that when one lies, one abandons the true Dharma and harms other people. The sutra says that lying is often the principal cause of many other serious transgressions, all of which bind one firmly to the cycle of birth and death. Lying obscures the truth and carries us farther and farther from it. Lies create innumerable obstacles to finding the way to liberation.

Buddhist literature recognizes lies of commission and lies of omission. When we say something that we know is not true we have committed an overt lie. When we fail to say something that we know we should say, we have committed a lie of omission. A lie of omission may be more subtle than an overt lie, but it is no less serious. If the intention is to harm someone or not prevent someone from harming themselves, a lie of omission can be extremely serious.

The *Upasakashila Sutra* says that frequent lying will produce in this life "harsh speech and an ugly appearance, and it will cause evil to accumulate around the liar, while no one will want to look on him." In his next life, the sutra says, the liar will "enter hell where he will suffer great hunger, thirst and heat." Following his long stay in hell, if the liar is reborn in the human realm, the sutra says he will "have poor speaking abilities and be mistrusted by others. People will not be happy to see him and even if he speaks the truth, they will not listen to him. He will live in poverty."

The *Dharmagupta Vinaya* distinguishes two basic forms of lying. To fabricate an untruth in general is called the "lesser form of lying." The "greater form of lying" mentioned in this text is the very serious offense of claiming to be enlightened when one is not.

Duplicity

Duplicity means to speak with a forked tongue. When we are duplicitous, we say one thing to this person and another thing to that person. If our intention in doing this is to create disharmony or confusion, we have committed a serious offense. Duplicity also means to pretend to have certain feelings while acting on the promptings of other, concealed feelings. When we deceive another person emotionally, we have committed a great offense against them.

A common form of duplicity is flattery. Flattery always is engaged in for ulterior reasons. Flattery is a form of trickery used to get someone to do something or give something they would not otherwise do or give. Whenever we smile falsely or use words to create false feelings among people, we are guilty of an offense against truth. Actions like these damage the natural trust that should prevail among groups of people.

The *Saddharma Smriti Upasthana Sutra* says, "Being too much attached to endless chattering leads to an increase of greed within oneself and an increase of fear in others. Duplicity is generally the result of the verbal transgressions of boasting and exaggerating."

The *Kushalamula Samgraha Sutra* says, "Harsh speech and duplicity are signs that one enjoys harming others or leading others to harm; being like this causes endless trouble."

The *Fayuan Chulin* says:

> Those who are duplicitous or who fight with others and cause discord among them will be torn in half once they fall into hell. They will have their mouths ripped out by the soldiers of hell and with heated knives their tongues will be cut away. They will suffer immensely and they will go hungry and be thirsty. They will not be able to free themselves from their evil karma. They will drink their own blood.

In another place the *Fayuan Chulin* says:

> When anyone harms another through an act of duplicity, he will definitely fall into one of the lower realms. If he does succeed in obtaining another human body, his bad karma will follow him everywhere; his family will be low-minded and evil and they will often fight with him and disagree with him and be angry and cause him trouble.

Duplicity creates disharmony within our small groups and it contributes to the general disharmony of the world. The mind that acts duplicitously is predominantly negative. A mind like this appears clever to itself while in reality it suffers from the ignorance of not knowing the full consequences of its actions. Duplicity is especially harmful if engaged in by practicing Buddhists. If we as Buddhists are hypocritical about our beliefs—if we profess one thing while doing another—we will only be working against the efforts of countless bodhisattvas and Buddhas. Rather than leading other sentient beings to the truth, our poor examples will be driving them away. It is very important that anyone interested in leading others to the Dharma always behave with honesty and straightforward sincerity.

Harsh speech

Harsh speech does not simply mean loud or forceful speech. Harsh speech is speech that hurts another person. Sometimes harsh speech can be conveyed through the subtlest tones of derision. Sometimes even rough words may not actually be harsh. If we are mindful, we should know when our words are intended to cause pain.

The *Introduction to the Stages of the Dharma Realm* says, "Evil words intended to bring suffering to another is what is meant by 'harsh speech.'"

The *Five-Part Vinaya* says:

> People are born with axes in their mouths and they cut themselves with their own harsh speech. They criticize those who should be praised and they praise those who should be criticized. The results of their behavior come back to them and thus they know no happiness.

Idle speech

The *Satyasiddhi Shastra* says that idle speech may be defined as any one of the following: untruthful speech, truthful speech that has been spoken at the wrong time, truthful speech that leads to someone's suffering, truthful speech that has no beginning or end, truthful speech that is disorganized or presented in an unreasonable manner.

The *Yogacharabhumi Shastra* says that idle speech can be defined as any one of the following: false speech, ill-timed speech, speech without significance, speech employing inaccurate terms, thoughtless speech, raucous speech, disorganized speech, pointless speech, speech with no larger meaning, speech that contradicts the Dharma.

Idle speech gives no value to others. It is a waste of time to listen to it. One who frequently engages in idle speech is in danger of creating senseless attachments to this world of delusion. Rambling or creative speech that has some higher goal in mind, of course, is not a form of idle speech.

> *If you want to achieve true contemplation,*
> *contemplate only name and form.*
> *If you want to achieve true realization,*
> *realize only name and form.*
> *Though you may choose to be ignorant*
> *and waste all of your time in thought,*
> *discriminating among myriad phenomena,*
> *still you will find nothing at all*
> *that reaches beyond name and form.*
>
> — from the *Mahaprajnaparamita Shastra*

Speech

Rough words harm both the self and others
while kind words bring benefit to all.

— from the *Sukhavativyuha Sutra*

The importance of speech
The importance of speech cannot be overemphasized. People create most of their bad karma through speech.

Speech is the single most powerful means by which we interact with other people. Our choice of words, our tone of voice, even our selection of subject matter can have the profoundest influence on other people. Intemperate or ill-considered speech often leads to misunderstanding, suspicion, and anger.

People become angry or suspicious because they are deluded. The "hook" that most often snags our delusive sense of self-existence is speech, and once it has been snagged we are more than likely to answer unkindly or become resentful. There is no simple cure for this problem. Just as we can easily offend others by what we say, they too can easily offend us with their speech. While we cannot control over what others say to us, we can listen to them with compassion and understanding and an intelligent willingness to tolerate their verbal excesses and their mistakes. At the same time, we can be careful of what we say to them.

Human psychology is revealed in our speech. It is good to remember that people who often speak angrily probably have a deep-seated need to do so. People who are frequently negative and critical probably speak that way because that is how they learned to talk; that is how people have always spoken to them. People who talk too much are probably doing so because deep down they feel that no one has ever listened to them. People who frequently say ignorant things simply don't know any better. If you are faced with someone like this, what is the most compassionate thing to do? Be patient, be tolerant, and don't compound the problem by adding speech mistakes of your own.

Lung Shu's Expanded Pure Land Treatise makes nine important points about how we should talk. Presented as metaphors, these points will help us use speech to create good karma and avoid the creation of bad karma. The *Treatise* says:

1) Whenever we chant the Buddha's name, our mouths are cleansed and the words that issue from them are like pearls.

2) Whenever we preach the Dharma, it is as if light were issuing from our mouths.

3) Whenever we speak uselessly or in a way that does no one any good, it is as if we were chewing on wood shavings.

4) Whenever we tease someone viciously, it is as if we were cutting them with a knife.

5) Whenever we use filthy speech, it is as if worms or bugs were crawling out of our mouths.

6) Whenever we speak of good things, it is as if a fragrance were coming from our mouths.

7) Whenever we speak truthfully and sincerely, it is as if our words were made of good silk cloth.

8) Whenever we deceive others, it is as if our words were the cover over a pit-trap.

9) Whenever we speak harshly or cruelly, it is as if a foul odor were coming from our mouths.

The dangers of harsh speech

Harsh speech is generally caused by anger. It is bad enough to allow ourselves to be angry, but as soon as we act on our anger to revile others we set off a series of events that may quickly explode out of control. Harsh, angry speech is like fire on a flammable surface. Anything can happen. At the very least, we will hurt someone else's feelings. At worst, our speech may cause violence.

The *Karmavibhanga Sutra* says:

> *If in this life you often use harsh speech to irritate others, and if you delight in exposing their private matters, and if you are stubborn and unyielding, then in your next life you will be born as a fire-spewing hungry ghost.*

The *Yogacharabhumi Sutra* says:

> *Ignorance and a hard heart produce words that are not soft and not warm. A person who is given to harsh and duplicitous speech will not think of what might benefit others and he will often speak recklessly and without ending. A person like this harbors evil in his heart much in the way ashes may cover a live fire; if you step on them you will burn your feet.*

The benefits of good speech

The practice of Buddhism requires that we focus our attention on the actions of our bodies and minds, and on our speech. Speech is so important to the successful practice of Buddhism that the Buddha accorded it the same prominence as the mind and the body. Speech can be like a handle that we use to take hold of all areas of our lives. When our speech is in keeping with the precepts of Buddhism, the rest of our behavior cannot be far behind.

The *Yogacharabhumi Sutra* says:

> *If your speech is always soft and agreeable and if it is in harmony with the feelings of others, then your behavior will be supported by it and you will not be likely to harm others through your body or mind. Good speech is like a flowering tree; in time its fruits will be sweet and beautiful.*

The *Diamond Sutra* says that Buddha is "the one of truthful words, of real words, the one who does not change what he has said and who does not lie."

The Buddha always spoke beautifully, honestly, and with great compassion and thus he was respected by everyone. The Buddha is our original teacher and he is the best example of how we should behave. If you have trouble knowing how to speak, try to imagine what the Buddha would say if he were in your situation. Remember, one of the Buddha's great characteristics was he was never frightening to people. Sometimes it is better just to be awkward or foolish than to strain to say something clever or insincere. It is always better to say something kind or encouraging than to speak sharply or derisively.

When Shakyamuni Buddha was still a bodhisattva, he was together with the bodhisattva Maitreya, who will be the next Buddha on earth. Shakyamuni became a Buddha before Maitreya largely because he expended more time and energy while still a bodhisattva in praising all the Buddhas in the universe. The power of his praise and the merits gained from his constant habit of good speech allowed him to reach full enlightenment before Maitreya.

The Buddha said that good speech generates ten kinds of merit. These ten are: a warm voice, fluent speech, the ability to reason well, beautiful speech, accurate speech, straightforward speech, fearless speech, respectful speech, the ability to speak well about the Dharma, and a good rebirth once this life is over.

In the end, we should try our best to be sure that our speech always is permeated with the wonderful energy we have gained from the Dharma. The beauty of the Dharma is capable of transforming us through our study of it and it is capable of changing others through the positive energy we take from it and then communicate to them.

We all learn the fastest when we learn from a Buddha. Even Shakyamuni Buddha learned in this way. When he was still a Bodhisattva he used his voice to recite the following verse for a period of seven days and seven nights:

Above Heaven, below Heaven
there is nothing and no one like the Buddha.
In all worlds, in all the ten directions
there is nothing to compare to him.
Nothing I have ever seen anywhere
can ever compare to him.

— from the *Abhiniskramana Sutra*

Overcoming Greed

Greed causes sadness;
greed causes fear.
If there is no greed,
how can there be sadness and fear?

— from the *Dharmapada*

The causes of greed

Greed is a basic disease of all sentient beings. In our realm, the desire realm (*kamadhatu*), the force and effects of greed can be felt especially strongly. Greed is based on ignorance and cannot function without it. The fundamental ignorance that enables greed to function is the belief in a self that exists separately and independently from other sentient beings. This belief leads to nothing but trouble. Once we believe we are separate, we begin to have desires, attachments, and the false certainty that we can obtain advantages for ourselves without including the well-being of others.

Greed springs from ignorance, and as it rears its ugly head, it causes more ignorance; the passions of greed and its myriad attachments always obscure higher awareness and they always weaken the moral sense.Greed has many names and many masks. Sometimes we call greed "wanting," sometimes we call it "love," sometimes we call it "needing," sometimes we call it "justice," and sometimes we call it "truth."

Greed is one of the six basic defilements (*klesha*) mentioned in Buddhist sutras. The six *klesha* are: greed, anger, ignorance, pride, doubt, and false views.

The *Yogacharabhumi Shastra* mentions the ten troubles (*anusaya*). The ten *anusaya* comprise a more detailed analysis of the forces that cause suffering among sentient beings. The ten *anusaya* are: greed, anger, pride, ignorance, doubt, identification with the body, nihilism or eternalism, disbelief in the laws of karma, self-righteousness, and excessive asceticism. In Chinese, the ten *anusaya* are called "the persistent sleep inducers" because any one of them can arise at any time and because their effects on us are to cloud our thinking and make us as if sleepy in the light of truth. The ten *anusaya* are seeds in the *alaya*-consciousness which we have planted ourselves sometime in the past.

Greed is also listed in the *Agamas* as one of the nine bonds that bind us to mortality (*bandhana*). The nine bonds of mortality are: love, hate, pride, ignorance, wrong views, greed, doubt, envy, meanness or selfishness.

The *Yogacharabhumi Shastra* says that greed arises from the five *skandha*. A human being is made up of five *skandha*, or "aggregates." These *skandha* are: form, feeling, perception, mental formation, and consciousness. The *Yogacharabhumi Shastra* says that ten conditions lead to greed. These conditions are: grasping; sight; not having; having; evil behavior; wanting to have children, friends, and relatives; the necessities of life; desire for eternal life; the desire not to have eternal life. Most of these conditions are normal aspects of our world. The *Yogacharabhumi Shastra* is not saying that these aspects should be avoided or despised; it is saying that these aspects or conditions can lead to greed if we become excessive in our attachments to them. Of course evil behavior need not be a normal aspect of life in this world.

We can begin analyzing the roots of greed by working backwards through the five *skandha*. First we become conscious of what greed is and how it affects us, then we begin to understand the mental formations which precede consciousness, then we begin to understand how our perceptions are conditioned by our expectations, then we begin to understand how our feelings predispose us to act as we do, and then lastly, we will begin to see form without desire.

The *Abhidharmakosha* says that there are four basic kinds of sexual greed:

1) Sexual greed inspired by physical coloring. This includes hair and skin color, make-up, clothing and so forth.

2) Sexual greed inspired by physical shape. This includes height, weight, beauty, appearance and so forth.

3) Sexual greed inspired by touch.

4) Sexual greed inspired by behavior and mannerisms. This includes all behavior, tone of voice, gesture and so forth.

The closer attention we pay to the origins and sources of greed, the sooner we will be able to suffuse these areas with a higher awareness that will ultimately grant us complete freedom from all attachment.

Problems caused by greed

Greed increases our attachments to this world, muddles our senses, and prevents us from perceiving the awesome fullness of the bodhi mind. When we first begin trying to give up greedy attachments, it may seem that we are losing more than we are gaining. As our wisdom grows, however, we will see that in truth we have given up nothing at all and have gained everything.

This world is made half of pleasure and half of pain. No matter what we do, we will experience some pain. If we allow ourselves to become attached to pleasure and become greedy for it, then that too will turn to pain someday. Greed has subtle ways of turning pleasure into sadness and drenching happiness with anxiety and fear. It is far better to allow life to flow where it must and not try to hang onto every little thing we think we must have.

In addition to the problems it causes in the present, greed plants seeds in the *alaya*-consciousness that strengthen all of our attachments to *samsara*. Look back over your life; you will be sure to see that your greed rarely has led you in the right direction. Now, consider your future; the greed you cannot control today will create the conditions of your future lives.

How to cure ourselves of greed

Greed must be controlled. However, if it is not controlled wisely, our very attempts to control it may lead to a subtler kind of greed. Buddhism is called the Middle Way because Buddhism teaches us to travel a path that lies midway between asceticism and worldliness. Through meditation, thoughtful introspection, and contemplation, all of us are capable of finding the wisdom necessary to overcome greed.

In the Theravadan tradition, people are generally advised to contemplate the fundamental impurities of desired objects in order to see through their attachments to them. In the Mahayana tradition, people are more often taught to contemplate the fundamental emptiness and impermanence of desired objects in order to see through their attachments to them. Both of these methods are very valuable.

The *Treatise on the Awakening of Faith in the Mahayana* explains that we should always seek to take the high road in everything we do. Tathagata, a name for Buddha, means "Thus-Come One." "Thusness" is reality as it is seen by a Buddha. The *Treatise on the Awakening of Faith in the Mahayana* says:

> *What should we tell sentient beings to help them get beyond the constant coming and going of mental processes so that they can gain access to full awareness of true thusness? We should tell them that all form and all phenomena have no intrinsic reality. And how is it that they have no intrinsic reality? Analyze form; gradually you will see that it is made of nothing more than fine dust. Then analyze this fine dust; you will see that it too is the same as all other forms: it is nothing more than images or reflections produced by the mental tendency to create distinctions. In reality, it does not exist.*
>
> *Apply this analysis to the other skandhas; gradually your thinking will take you to the smallest unit of time, a ksana. From the point of view of a ksana it can be seen that no form or phenomena is a single, complete entity.*
>
> *Even the uncaused states [asamskrita dharmas: i.e. space, passionlessness, effortless cessation] are like this.*

Therefore, simply disentangling yourself from the realm of phenomena will not bring you full awareness of true thusness.

All dharmas, all laws, and all phenomena throughout the entire universe are the same. They are all like this. One should understand this point completely for this is how phenomena delude people. No matter where you turn the truth is always the same. And no matter where you turn sentient beings allow themselves to be deluded in the same ways. Only the mind can be moved or disturbed: the truth never moves.

If you understand how the mind moves and how thoughts come and go, then you will gain access to full awareness of true thusness.

A life without greed

Greed is without essence.
All attachment is illusion.

— from the *Yogacharabhumi Shastra*

In the end, a life without greed is achieved simply by realizing that greed has no fundamental reality; that there is no one to be greedy and there is nothing to be greedy about. Once we fully understand this truth, we will be beyond all greed. The wisdom of the bodhi mind easily transcends any and all attachments to this *saha* world.

One who follows these teachings
becomes as brilliant as the sun and moon
and he can overcome all darkness.

— from the *Lotus Sutra*

Ending Anger

Returning anger with anger is evil.
Don't return anger with anger.
Not being angry is always better
than being angry.

— from the *Samyukta Agama*

The origins of anger

Anger is one of the three basic "poisons" discussed by the Buddha. Ignorance and greed are the other two. Generally, the Three Poisons operate together. They feed off each other, justify each other and create the conditions which lead to their malefic reappearances. They create the karma that binds us to the lower awareness typical of this *saha* world. The Three Poisons are sometimes also called "the three fires" because they make our minds burn and rage with ignorance like a fire out of control. Sometimes they are also called "the three diseases" because they bring harm to sentient beings and force them to remain long within the cycle of birth and death.

The *Abhidharmakosha* and the *Vijnaptimatratasiddhi Shastra* both say that anger is a condition in which the mind roils with trouble and cannot find peace because it has turned its back on wisdom and its claws against others. Anger comes in many forms: resentment, hatred, jealousy, cruelty, abuse, taking delight in the misfortunes of others. Anger has many names, but essentially it is always caused by a deluded belief that the illusory self has lost control over something that is important to it. This loss of control produces an ignorant rage during which we attempt to restore whatever equilibrium we thought should have been there. If this rage happens in the moment, we call it anger or fury. If it burns more slowly over a longer period of time, we call it hatred or jealousy or resentment. The cause is always the same; the illusion has been threatened and rather than learn it elects to harm.

The Buddha said that anger was one of the Five Hindrances. The Five Hindrances are moods or states of mind that make it difficult for us to learn the Dharma. They are anger, desire, drowsiness, excitability, and doubt. The Buddha also said that anger is one of the Five Envoys of Stupidity. The Five Envoys of Stupidity are greed, anger, ignorance, pride, and doubt.

Buddhism recognizes three basic kinds of anger:

1) Anger for no reason. This form of anger arises within the mind even though nothing has come from outside to provoke it. This kind of anger grows out of seeds already planted within the *alaya*-consciousness.

2) Anger with some reason. This form of anger arises after someone has done something to "cause" it. This kind of anger is produced when a seed of anger in the *alaya*-consciousness is stimulated to grow by outer conditions.

3) Dialectical anger. This form of anger arises when someone disagrees with us. It is produced in the same way as anger with some reason.

Anger is a form of suffering peculiar to the realm of desire (*kama-dhatu*). In *rupadhatu* (the realm of form) and *arupadhatu* (the realm of formlessness) there is no anger.

Anger is distinguished from greed in that anger is a form of revulsion created by something we do not like, while greed is a form of attraction brought on by something we do like. In this limited sense, and in this sense only, greed can be said to be "better than" anger. Greed at least has some positive components while anger generally has none at all.

Anger as transgression

The *Avatamsaka Sutra* says, "Of all forms of evil, there is none worse than anger. A single moment of anger can be an enormous obstruction to growth."

The *Fayuan Chulin* says, "Anger causes the loss of all goodness as it causes the beginning of all evil. Anger ruins the joy of the Dharma, steals the goodness of the mind, and forces the mouth to say terrible things. Anger is like the blade of an ax."

Anger is one of the greatest obstructions to the successful study of Buddhism. Anger is a form of passionate ignorance. It is hard enough to learn when we are simply ignorant, but how can we ever learn if we are passionate in our ignorance? Only a quiet and receptive mind can learn. A mind raging with fire only burns its own fuel. For this reason, Buddha often counseled his followers to beware of anger. All of us must learn to control and overcome anger.

The *Sutra of Bequeathed Teachings* says:

> Anger can ruin all good practices and it is not soon
> forgotten. It is attractive neither in the present nor when
> viewed later as something belonging to the past. When
> anger begins burning out of control like a raging fire,
> protect yourself and do not let it consume you. Like a
> thief this fire will take away everything you have. There
> is nothing worse than anger.

The *Mahaprajnaparamita Shastra* says:

> Anger should be thought of as the worst of all
> transgressions. It is the worst of all the Three Poisons.
> Of the ninety-eight defilements, it is the most stubborn.
> It is the most difficult mental disease of all to cure.
> A person in the midst of anger cannot see what is right;
> he understands neither the difference between good and
> evil nor the difference between helping and hurting. He
> has lost control of himself and begun to fall toward the
> hell realm.

The *Saddharma Smriti Upasthana Sutra* says that anger is like a poisonous snake, like a knife blade, like fire. The sutra says that wise people should do all they can to overcome anger.

The *Bodhisattvabhumi Shastra* says that anyone who is often angry will almost certainly fall into one of the lower three realms of existence (hell, hungry ghosts, animals). If they are reborn in the human realm then they will suffer both of the following two problems: 1) they will often be victims of other people's fault-finding and criticism, and 2) they will often be troubled and bothered by other people and will find little or no peace in their lives.

The cure for anger

Anger is a form of energy. The most basic way to cure anger is to see it that way. Remove all labels from it and disentangle it from all stories or excuses about why it is there. Seen purely as energy, anger is more easily put in perspective and controlled. Another way to control anger is to consider times in the past when you were angry. What do they matter now? Did they really matter then? After enough time has past, recalling anger is like recalling the heat of a fire. There is a memory but no feeling.

The *Mahaprajnaparamita Shastra* says:

> Overcoming anger brings peace to the mind. Overcoming
> anger leads to a mind without regrets. Anger is the source
> of the poisons that destroy goodness. All the Buddhas
> praise one who has overcome anger. When anger has
> been overcome, there no longer will be any anxiety.

The *Saddharma Smriti Upasthana Sutra* says that one who overcomes anger is loved by all and is delightful to see. His mind is calm, his face is pure and he is trusted by everyone. Once anger has been overcome, the sutra says, it follows naturally that one will be successful in upholding the precepts and in controlling fear, passion, criticism, harsh speech, and a tendency to complain or be bitter about one's life. Overcoming anger is the source of much goodness. The merits which accrue to anyone who has overcome this vice lead to good circumstances in this life and a good rebirth after this life is over.

The *Mahayana Samparigraha Shastra* mentions five ways to overcome anger:

1) Contemplate that since beginningless time you have been connected with all sentient beings in the universe.

2) Contemplate the transience of life. Who is there to be harmed and who is doing the harming?

3) Contemplate that only the Dharma is real and that there is no such thing as sentient beings. In this light, how can there be any such thing as harm?

4) Contemplate that all sentient beings must suffer. In this light, why would anyone want to increase the suffering of another?

5) Contemplate that all sentient beings are your children. Why would you want to harm any of them?

When all is said and done, compassion is the single best method for overcoming anger. The bodhisattva must learn to "be compassionate for no reason and to see all beings as being of one body."

If anger rises and you desire
to harm another being,
already you have harmed
yourself far more than him.
And that is why you must
often think on compassion;
for compassion keeps from rising
all thought of anger, evil, and pain.

— from the *Meditation on the Three Contemplations Sutra*

Knowing How to be Satisfied

If you do not know how to be satisfied,
even if you are rich you will be poor.
If you do know how to be satisfied,
even if you are poor you will be rich.

— from the *Sutra of Bequeathed Teachings*

Excessive desire

Desire is the most basic bond that binds us to the delusions of this world. Due to our desires we are born over and over again in one of the six realms of existence.

The *Mahaprajnaparamita Shastra* says that desires kindle feelings of dissatisfaction from start to finish. When we begin to desire something, we feel dissatisfied because we do not yet have it. If we get it, we feel dissatisfied because it has not lived up to our expectations or because we now fear that we may lose it. After we have lost it or after it has grown old we feel dissatisfied again. If we are wise we will take heed of this inevitable process.

The great poet Su Tung-p'o said, "Human desires are boundless and endless, but the capacity of objects to satisfy our desires is not."

The Avadanas say, "Even if the seven treasures were to rain down from heaven they still would not satisfy desire. Desire gives rise to few pleasures and many troubles. To understand this truth is to be a sage."

The *Sutra of Bequeathed Teachings* says:

> *People with many desires are always looking for gain and
> thus they suffer and have many troubles. People with few
> desires feel no need to lust after things and thus they are
> peaceful and free of many troubles.*

When the sutras talk about desires in this way they are talking
about desires for things we do not need. The desire for a drink of
water when you are thirsty is not going to bind you to this world. The
desire to own a swimming pool and sip lemonade beside it when you
are thirsty, however, will bind you to this world.

The joy of knowing how to be satisfied with what you have
Knowing how to be satisfied with what we have is a very important
starting point for the successful practice of Buddhism. We should
look upon what we have with a more or less neutral sense of
satisfaction. Our possessions should not lead us to feel shame or
guilt or desire. If we truly have a need to acquire something we do
not have, we should pursue that need level-headedly and without the
imbalanced feeling that we must have whatever it is immediately and
without delay.

Needs should not be confused with desires. Once our basic needs
have been met we should allow our consciousness to roam freely
within the glory of existence and the beauty of the Dharma. Don't
burden yourself with useless desires that can only lead you away
from the truth. As Buddhists, our primary area of concern is the
mind and not the material world.

The *Bodhisattva Gocharopaya Visaya Vikurvana Nirdesha Sutra* says:

> *People who are greedy are always trying to accumulate
> things and then even when they get them they are not
> satisfied. Their thinking is disturbed and full of igno-
> rance and this state leads them to prey on others and
> often think of how to gain advantages over them. Their
> behavior produces resentment and anger in this life and
> once they die they will be reborn in the evil realms. The*

> *wise understand these consequences and thus they learn*
> *how to be satisfied with whatever they have.*

The *Avadanas* say, "Knowing how to be satisfied is the best good fortune."

The *Eight Realizations of the Bodhisattva Sutra* says:

> *A mind which does not know how to be satisfied, but*
> *always wants more and more, only adds to its misfortune*
> *and trouble. The bodhisattva is not like that. The bodhi-*
> *sattva knows how to be satisfied; he is peaceful in poverty*
> *and able to uphold the way. His only desire is to become*
> *wise.*

The world of one who is satisfied

Our minds are the world. When our minds know how to experience a sense of sufficiency in all circumstances, we are free. Beyond distinctions, beyond greed, beyond the lusts that impel us toward yet another embrace with delusion, the mind that knows how to be satisfied rests in the equality of complete truth. Such a mind has no need to make comparisons, it does not calculate, it does not suffer, and it does not experience pain. Once the mind achieves this state, it understands that everything in the universe already belongs to it; the birds, the flowers, the stars in the sky, the rippling of running water—all of it is the mind and all of it belongs to the mind. Where is the need for possessiveness or greed then?

Yen Hui, an imperturbable disciple of Confucius, was described by his master as 'living in mean quarters, with simple food and drink, in a state which most people would despise, and yet he was full of joy.'

Mahakashyapa, one of Buddha's disciples, spent years living in remote graveyards as part of his ascetic practice, and yet he did not feel as if he were suffering or as if his life were lacking in anything.

The Japanese Zen master Ryokan (1758–1831) lived "with a little grain in a sack and a little wood by his stove." Nevertheless, he "sat cross-legged and at ease in his thatch hut under the rain." He was always satisfied and would have been perplexed by the idea of wanting anything to be different than it was.

Today, it is difficult to live as simply as people in the past did, for they lived in slow-paced agricultural societies. Modern societies are complex technological achievements that require a much higher level of activity just to maintain basic needs. While we can no longer copy the lifestyles of the sages of the past, we can learn much from their spirits. The spirit of people like Ryokan or Yen Hui was one of acceptance, equanimity and deep satisfaction. Those of us who are alive today may have to make car payments and housing payments and we may have to juggle many complex factors just to maintain ourselves, but we can still live in a way that honors a basic trust in the flow of life and that gives us basic satisfaction with whatever we have. We can still live with our feet on the ground and our heads in the sky.

How to be satisfied with what you have

Since desire is incapable of producing satisfaction, it follows that we cannot cure a sense of dissatisfaction through desire. Dissatisfaction must be overcome by wisdom and by helping others. If our minds are in the habit of always chasing one desire after another, we must force ourselves to recognize this and understand what we are doing. Once consciousness is turned to any area of our lives, a change for the better cannot be far behind.

The *Mahaprajnaparamita Shastra* says that one way to overcome desire is to realize that desires need a seed within and a stimulant without. These two aspects go together. When we begin to feel an untoward desire, the *shastra* says, we should examine both the seed within and the stimulant without. Then we should consider that they are mutually interdependent; there cannot be one without the other. Having understood that, the *shastra* then says we should disentangle ourselves from both factors at once. The *shastra* says that we should remove the seed within while simultaneously turning away from the stimulant without.

Desires can also be overcome by considering their consequences, the amount of time they cause us to waste, their inherent emptiness, and the time they steal from the much more important work of studying the Dharma and improving ourselves. Whenever we overcome a desire, we experience an increase in energy and understanding. The level of our consciousness is raised by just that much every time we turn our gaze away from a low attachment.

If we have tried the above techniques and still failed to overcome our desires, we should redouble our efforts to help others. The bodhisattva helps himself primarily through his willingness to help others. When we focus our attention more on the needs of others and less on our own desires, we will go a long way toward seeing beyond the delusive mirage of greed and desire.

When one seeks an object of desire,
one suffers.
When one gets an object of desire,
one fears losing it.
When one loses an object of desire,
one is greatly troubled.
At each and every point,
there is no joy.

If all desire causes suffering like this,
then how is one to be rid of it?
One can rid oneself of desire
by learning the joys of samadhi
found in deep meditation.

— from the *Mahaprajnaparamita Shastra*

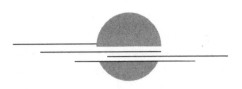

Evil is a Thief

Evil springs from the mind;
then it turns on the mind and robs it.
Evil is like rust on iron;
slowly it destroys the form.

—from the *Fo Shuo Pei Sutra*

The *Mahaparinirvana Sutra* says:

> *The mind controls the body. The body does not control*
> *the mind. The mind can fool the body and it can kill the*
> *body. The mind can choose to be an Arhant or it can*
> *choose to be in Heaven. It can choose to be a person, an*
> *animal, an insect, a wild bird, or it can choose to be in*
> *hell. The mind can choose to be a hungry ghost and it*
> *can choose the appearance of its body. The mind can do*
> *anything.*

In a mere moment our minds are capable of taking us from heaven to hell and back again. The basis of the mind is Buddha nature. In our deepest "selves" all of us are Buddhas already. However, due to the defilements of greed, anger, and ignorance our minds are deluded; rather than enjoy liberation in the resplendent truth of the Tathagata, they seek their own bondage in the delusions of *samsara*.

As soon as we decide to overcome our ignorance by striving to realize our Buddha nature, we will begin to overcome the defilements

that bind us to delusion. Once this change occurs within us, our
minds will become our greatest allies and not our greatest enemies.
Rather than lead us away from the truth, they will begin to lead us
toward the Buddha with every thought we think and everything we
feel. Such is the joy of Buddhism and the joy of learning the Dharma.

Use the mind's goodness to overcome its evil

When the Buddha spoke about the mind, he meant all acts of
sentience or potential sentience, including thought, emotion,
perception, movement of the body, desires, instincts, basic proclivi-
ties, basic tendencies and so forth. All of these functions and aspects
are fundamentally functions and aspects of the mind as this word is
used in Buddhism.

Our minds are characterized by their changeability and by their
tendency to leap from one emotion or idea to another. In the mind
good mixes with bad, and if we are not careful, our attention will be
guided by fascination more than by truth or by what is best for us.
The Buddha said that his teachings are like medicine because they
are able to cure us of our chronic misuse of the mind. The Buddha
compared the Dharma to water because it is able to cleanse the mind
of its defilements.

The Dharma should be our basic tool for overcoming the evil tendencies of the mind. By constantly exposing ourselves to the wisdom
of the Dharma, we will gradually learn to actively value truth and
morality over delusion and indulgence.

The Dharma helps us reveal to ourselves the Buddha who lives
within us at all times. Inklings of the purity and perfection of this
indwelling Buddha nature are manifested in the mind as faith,
morality, and a desire to help others. We can best learn to overcome
evil tendencies by allowing ourselves to be instructed by the purity
of the Buddha within us. Once we have seen how much better it is
to do good than to do evil, we will begin to have even greater trust in
our own inherent goodness. Once this trust becomes fully developed, the possibility of being drawn into evil thinking will be greatly
reduced. The warm glow of the Buddha within can only grow
brighter and warmer as we learn to rely on it more and more.

The *Avatamsaka Sutra* mentions ten characteristics of the mind of a bodhisattva. When one's intuitive comprehension of the Buddha within has grown to absolute certainty, one's mind will be bathed in these ten good qualities. They are: helping others, compassion, peaceful joy, steadiness, comforting others, concentration, protecting others, feeling that others are part of oneself, having the ability to teach, and having the ability to lead others to the good.

No sooner do we overcome our own selfish delusions than we must realize that the delusions and selfishness of others are ours too. All sentient beings are one with us and all of them deserve our finest attention. When we focus on others and really try to help them, we also help ourselves.

How to use the mind to overcome doubt

Doubt is one of the most basic of all of the defilements. Many tragedies happen only because one person doubted another. When friends doubt each other, often their friendship is irreparably harmed. When husbands and wives begin to doubt each other, the forces of love and caring which brought them together quickly begin to weaken. Doubt chains us to our own mistakes and contorts everything that we do. Doubt is a poison that pollutes every thought that rises around it. Doubt ruins communications between people as it demeans both the self and others at once.

The way to overcome doubt, as with all defilement, is to assert its opposite, positive quality. When we find ourselves becoming suspicious or doubtful, we should turn our minds toward trust and a firm belief in the truth. This does not mean that we should allow ourselves to be abused by other people, but it does mean that we should not abuse them ourselves through unwarranted suspicion. If you find that you have a tendency to become suspicious of others, it is good to remember that what they do will produce their karma and what you do will produce your karma. If their behavior really is bad, it will not harm you if you have been trusting. If their behavior really was good, it will harm you if you have not been trusting.

At its deepest levels trust is an aspect of the Buddha mind, which knows already that everything is just as it should be and that nothing whatsoever needs our interference, much less our anger, suspicion or doubt.

The worst form of doubt is doubt in the Buddha. If we do not believe that the Buddha spoke the truth, we will not study the Dharma and we will not be able to make any progress in this life. The surest cure for this kind of doubt is study the Dharma and apply it in your life. No one who studies the Dharma and applies it in his life will doubt it for long.

The *Mahasamnipata* says, "The greatest and most beautiful form of wisdom is to be beyond doubt."

The *Mahaprajnaparamita Shastra* says, "The Dharma is a great ocean which we enter by faith and cross by the power of wisdom."

> *All suffering and all defilement*
> *are nothing but delusion.*
> *They have no self-nature of their own*
> *and they persist from beginningless time*
> *only because they have not yet established*
> *meaningful interaction with theTathagatagharba.*

— from the *Treatise on the Awakening of Faith in the Mahayana*

How to cure the mind of pettiness and intolerance

Small-mindedness is the antithesis of the Buddha mind. Being small-minded can be likened to looking through the wrong end of a telescope: the obvious becomes hard to see, while the greatness of all of life is lost in a selected detail. One of the best reasons to study the Dharma every day is the Dharma has the ability to open our minds, to stretch them and to expand them to their greatest potential. Why hold yourself back? Why be intolerant when you can be large-minded?

The *Avatamsaka Sutra* compares the mind of a bodhisattva to a great and expansive land which can hold all beings and nurture all forms of life. The sutra also compares the mind of a bodhisattva to a great ocean which constantly is being infused with the even greater wisdom and compassion of all of the Buddhas.

Our true mind is as vast as all space, brighter than the sun, and as wise as all of the Buddhas in the universe. Why settle for less? That mind is yours. It is your inheritance and it is the source of your being. You can only keep yourself from it by willful acts of pettiness and closed-mindedness. Recognition of this truth coupled with sincere study of the Dharma will eventually cure the mind of all narrow tendencies.

The *Fo Shuo Pei Sutra* says:

> *There are four basic ways that you can hurt yourself in this world. The first is to break off the branch of your own tree when it is flowering and laden with fruit. The second is to act like a poisonous snake which bites itself. The third is to act like a dishonest official who harms his own country. The fourth is to not be a good person and thus be reborn in hell.*

We can always cure negative tendencies by asserting their positive opposites while keeping in mind the examples set for us by Shakyamuni Buddha and the great bodhisattvas. At the same time it is a very good practice to contemplate often the Four Immeasurable States of Mind of the Tathagata: boundless kindness, boundless compassion, boundless joy and boundless equanimity.

> *Avalokiteshvara Bodhisattva is compassion.*
> *Mahasthamaprapta Bodhisattva is joyful renunciation.*
> *Sakyamuni Buddha is complete purity.*
> *Maitreya Bodhisattva is equanimity.*
>
> — from the *Platform Sutra of the Sixth Patriarch*

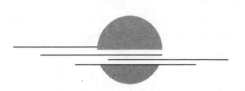

A Good Reputation

Do not speak of others' faults
and do not talk of your own virtues.
Wisely contemplate the oneness and equality
of all sentient beings
and you will enjoy a good reputation.

— from the *Sutra on the Principles of the Six Paramitas*

Do not speak of others' faults

We should always try to see the good in others, not the bad. On the samsaric level of this *saha* world alone, backbiting and faultfinding are known by most people to be totally counterproductive. Not only does faultfinding produce nothing but anger and mistrust, but the effects of negative speech also create an environment in which it becomes difficult to do anything positive.

Negativity and excessive criticism lead nowhere but downhill. Usually people engage in these practices out of feelings of jealousy, anger, or low self-esteem. If you find yourself behaving this way, bite your tongue and seriously reflect on your behavior at the first convenience. Once you become sensitive to the enormous problems caused by faultfinding, you will be much less prone to engage in it again. Having encouraged sensitivity on this subject, let me quickly add that oversensitivity toward criticism made of you is to be avoided at all costs. This is the bodhisattva way; we are gentle with others no matter what. We do not violate them, and if they should violate us, we do not feel disturbed.

Do not talk of your own virtues

The bodhisattva seeks to live perfectly within the inherent equality of all life. He does not attack others and he is not proud of himself. This is balance. This is equanimity. Just as we should not be negative toward others in what we say, so we should never allow ourselves to sing our own praises. If you have any virtues at all, they will be noticed by others. Let others praise you if there must be praise, but do not praise yourself.

Wisely contemplate the oneness and equality of all sentient beings

When you are able to do this, you will be beyond all praise and blame. You will see that there is no such thing as praise or blame. The gaze of one who is compassionate can see this, for compassion is the highest wisdom. In the depths of compassion we become aware that there are no differences among the myriad sentient beings of this vast universe. The Buddha mind, the Bodhi mind, the minds of sentient beings are the same. In this consciousness, all dualities merge into the universal truth. In this consciousness:

> Language is gone
> The mind is still
> Without beginning
> Without end
> This is Nirvana.
> All else is the
> Way of the world.
> Only this is the
> Highest Siddhanta.

—from the *Mahaprajnaparamita Shastra*

Repentance

All sin is like frost on the ground;
when the wisdom sun rises, it's gone.
This is why with all our hearts we must
repent the failings of our six senses.

— from the *Samantabhadrotsahana Parivarta Sutra*

All "sin" is fundamentally empty

"Humans are not saints; how can they be expected to live without transgression?" This ancient saying is a good place to begin this discussion. Like illness, transgression or sin is an inevitable part of human life. Hardly a day goes by when most of us don't do something wrong; most of us violate the precepts of body, mouth, or mind almost constantly. A "normal" human life is full of lying, stealing, cheating, intemperance, and excessive sensuality. Even if we learn to achieve some control over our bodies and mouths, most of us continue to violate the deeper sense of the precepts through improper thoughts like jealousy, anger, envy, resentment, or greed.

This brief summary of the facts of life is not meant to encourage bad behavior! It is only meant to help us arrive at a balanced and reasonable appraisal of human existence. As we labor to understand and improve ourselves, let us always remember:

Bad karma is empty in itself,
a product merely of mind.

When the mind is quiet,
sin is forgotten.
When the mind is forgotten
and sins are quiet then
both have attained emptiness;
and this is what is called
true repentance.

— from the *Avatamsaka Sutra*

To be human is to err. When we have erred, we must try to correct ourselves and not repeat the same mistake again. Transgressions are to be understood and corrected, not dwelt upon or agonized over. The transgressions we leave behind are like highway posts that mark our progress. The *Avatamsaka Sutra* says:

All bad karma that I created in the past
was created from beginningless
greed, anger or ignorance.
It was born from acts of body,
mouth or mind.
And now I repent it all.

The significance of repentance

Repentance is an important part of Buddhist practice. Zen masters often say, "Fear not the appearance of the thought; fear tardy observation of the thought."

"Observation of the thought" means introspection or reflection on the workings of our own minds. This saying means that we should never fear any thought; what we should fear is entertaining an evil thought, or worse, acting on one. Thoughts flow through the mind constantly. A Buddhist should never be afraid of any thought, for all thoughts are empty.

"Observation of the thought" or constantly reflecting on one's thoughts is the basic act of repentance. A wise bodhisattva knows that the future is produced in the present. He knows that karmic retribution is caused by evil intent. By constantly observing his thoughts, he disengages himself from the tendency to allow untoward thoughts to grow into the demons of evil intention. Observation of thought is fundamental to successful practice of Buddhism.

In Chinese the word repentance (*ch'an-hui*) is a combination of two words. The richer meaning of this combination might be rendered in English by using the combination "penitence-repentance." There is a subtle but important distinction between these two words in English, as in Chinese. "Penitence" emphasizes the state of mind of one who deeply recognizes his transgression and is determined not to repeat it. "Repentance" emphasizes the change of mind and the determination not to repeat the transgression.

The *Platform Sutra of the Sixth Patriarch* says:

> *When one is penitent, one regrets one's transgressions.
> One regrets the causes of bad karma. One regrets one's
> ignorance and confusion, one's pride, one's envy, one's
> jealousy and everything else one has done in error. When
> all of one's transgressions are intimately regretted in all of
> their details and when one is beyond ever doing them
> again, this is what is called penitence.*
>
> *When one is repentant, one has awakened. One is
> determined never to repeat the transgressions of the past.
> One is determined to disentangle oneself from all sources
> of bad karma, from ignorance and confusion, from pride,
> from envy, from jealousy and everything else one has
> done in error. When one is determined to disentangle
> oneself completely from all transgression, then one can
> be said to be repentant.*
>
> *This is the meaning of penitence-repentance* (ch'an-hui).

It is very important to understand that Buddhism is not focused on mistakes or making people feel guilty about mistakes they have made. Buddhism is focused on correcting mistakes. Mistakes must be recognized and they must be repented. Once they have been corrected they should not be dwelt upon anymore. Excessive guilt and remorse are false attachments just as much as greed and jealousy are.

Penitence is fundamental to Buddhism for it is the very crux of the mental and emotional change all Buddhists must be willing to undergo. Without penitence and shame we will become arrogant and our growth will be warped. Having said this, it is important to say as well that penitence is not a gloomy, masochistic sense of guilt that stalks us like a shadow for years. Ultimately everything is empty. We learn and grow by recognizing our mistakes and moving on.

Penitence is like Dharma water, for it cleanses us. It is like a raft, for it can take us to the other shore. Penitence is like medicine, because it can cure us of our ills. It is like a lamp in the darkness, for it can show us our way when before we saw nothing at all. Penitence is like a wall around a city, for it can protect our minds and our senses from being violated by the bandits of passion and greed. Penitence is like a bridge, for it helps us cross over our difficulties and enter upon the path of Buddhism with relative ease. Penitence is like a beautiful ornament which can decorate and make the Bodhi Way seem even more magnificent.

The *Sutra in Forty-Two Sections* says, "If there is evil, it must be recognized. Once evil has been corrected, good will be the result. As evil is lessened, one will come to see the truth."

The *Ts'ai Ken T'an* says, "Even the greatest transgressions can be repented."

In the *Five-Part Vinaya*, the Buddha says, "In the practice of my Dharma, recognition of transgressions and repentance of them will lead to an increase in goodness."

In this statement, the Buddha is saying that not only will repentance lessen the bad karma caused by our transgression, but it will also increase our basic goodness.

How to repent

Many different methods of repentance are mentioned in the Buddhist sutras. The *Samantabhadrotsahana Parivarta Sutra* says:

> You should repent the actions of your body and mind. Of the body: repent acts of killing, robbery, and intemperance. Of the mind: repent all evil thoughts and the ten

evil deeds and the five hellish acts. The mind is like a
wild ape. Or it is like glue in that it sticks to everything
through its greed and through the operation of the six
senses. The roots of the six senses give rise to the branch-
es and leaves that proliferate throughout the three
realms. The roots of the six senses give rise to ignorance,
old age and death. They give rise to the cycle of birth and
death and all manner of hardship and trouble. You
should repent the actions of your body and mind.

The *Samantabhadrotsahana Parivarta Sutra* mentions six means of assuring proper repentance throughout our lives. They are:

1) Have repentant eyes: Evil often begins in the eye. First we see something, then evil thoughts arise. By watching over ourselves and our responses to what we see, we can begin to gain control of this very significant source of bad behavior. By being careful about the thoughts that arise from what we see, we can succeed in not creating a great deal of bad karma.

2) Have repentant ears: The ears can be a source of many disturbing and unsettling sounds. Some kinds of sounds have the power to encourage improper behavior or improper thoughts. When we find ourselves being disturbed by sounds like this, it is good to consider their inherent emptiness. Sound is a good access point to understanding emptiness since sound is so manifestly transient and insubstantial.

3) Have a repentant nose: Many of our physical appetites are stimulated by smells. If we find ourselves being led toward gluttony or intemperance by odors in the air, we should stop and consider how our mind is being moved like an animal's mind, thoughtlessly and without any consideration of consequences.

4) Have a repentant tongue: Our tongues are one of the finest means we have for expressing ourselves. At the same time, the power of the tongue can also be turned toward evil. Most bad karma is created by speech. Watch your tongue carefully and be sure that it is always being used with compassion and intelligence.

5) Have a repentant mind: The basic activity of the untrained mind is as wild and disorganized as a drunken monkey. It jumps from

here to there for no reason and forgets where it came from before it arrives. If we want to control our minds, we must contemplate the Buddha and practice his Dharma at all times. Constant close observation of the workings of the mind is an indispensable technique for growth in Buddhism.

6) Have a repentant body: All of the temptations and desires of life play out through our bodies. The mind is the source, but the body is the means. If we have failed to control our minds, our bodies will move in the wrong direction; we will find ourselves close to the point of wrong-doing. Stop there. It is still not too late. The mind rules and in this last instant before a transgression has been committed, it can still stop the body in its tracks. In time, you will see how much better it was to have stopped.

Contemplation, meditation and chanting are excellent means to increase the power of the mind to observe itself and control itself. All of Buddhism works together to help us advance. The whole Dharma is on your side the moment you decide to change for the better.

Penitence and repentance save us from our lower urges and help us rise to the highest levels of consciousness.

> Our evil deeds of the past
> are like clouds over the moon.
> The decision to change
> it is like a torch in the dark.

— from the *Adbhutadharma Sutra*

Listening to the Dharma

When Ananda saw the Buddha,
he prostrated himself before him and wept;
and he felt a beginningless remorse
and an endless craving to hear the Dharma
for he knew his understanding
still was not complete.

— from the *Shurangama Sutra*

We cannot learn the Dharma deeply unless we listen to it, read about it and study it very often. Even Ananda, who heard the Buddha speak more than anyone else, craved the Dharma. His desire to learn was so great it caused him to weep at the sight of his Master.

If Ananda himself could feel like that, then how should those of us who call ourselves Buddhists today feel about the Dharma? Should we not daily recognize the treasure that has been bequeathed to us? And should we not daily turn to it to learn? For a moment imagine the world without the Dharma.

Practicing Buddhists all should try to spend at least some time every day reading Dharma literature or listening to someone speak about the Dharma. The levels of meaning contained in the Dharma are truly wonderful and no one will ever be able to fully appreciate them without frequently studying Buddhist literature. We cannot expect to progress unless we frequently expose ourselves to the immense wisdom contained in the Buddha's teachings.

Thus have I heard

All Buddhist sutras begin with the phrase, "Thus have I heard." The practice called "listening to the Dharma" takes its name from the very early days of Buddhism when the Buddha's teachings were transmitted orally. In those days, the only way to learn the Dharma was through listening to someone speak about it from memory. When we use the phrase "listening to the Dharma" today, we should expand its meaning to include reading, watching movies about Buddhism, or engaging in other activities that promote increased understanding of the Dharma.

Just as a plant needs water and sunlight to grow, so a Buddhist practitioner needs regular and constant exposure to the Dharma to progress. There can be no growth in Buddhism if we stop listening to the Dharma and stop trying to find deeper and deeper meanings in it. Even the greatest bodhisattvas listen to the Dharma constantly.

And even ghosts can benefit from listening to the Dharma. In the *Samyukta Agama* there is a story about an occasion when the Buddha preached the Dharma to a family of ghosts. Two young ghosts were so moved by the experience that they wept. Their mother, who was also present, said to them, "Since I listened to the Dharma, I became aware of its truth. If you will only do the same, then you will see its truth too."

In the *Mahaparinirvana Sutra* the Buddha says:

> *What constitutes insufficient listening [to the Dharma]?*
> *The Tathagata preached twelve kinds of sutras; if you only listen to six of them while ignoring the other six, that would be insufficient listening. And even if you practiced six of these kinds of sutras but were unable to chant them or explain them to others, that too would constitute insufficient listening because your understanding would not be bringing you or anyone else any good.*
> *Furthermore if you merely treated these six kinds of sutras as essays, or if you only used them to appear better than others, or if you only used them for mundane gain, or if you were possessive about them, even if you were*

able to chant them and explain them, still your listening
would be insufficient.

Good monks, the sutras contain complete teachings
which can be learned only through complete listening.

True, deep human understanding is based on what we do and the
kinds of feedback we provide ourselves with. Our growth will be
assured if we frequently study the Dharma. If we allow ourselves to
stop learning, then our understanding will begin to ossify while our
ability to practice will decline.

The Dharma is like water. It can wash us clean, but it must be
used often.

Humility

True listening requires that we be receptive, and true receptivity
requires that we be humble. If we begin with the idea that we already
know what the Buddha is saying, we will be unlikely to learn anything from him. If we are humble when we read the Dharma, we will
discover that a passage which meant one thing yesterday has
revealed a whole new level of meaning today. The teachings of the
Buddha are carried on the backs of words, but their true significance
is far deeper than anything any word can express. For this reason, the
Dharma is capable of constantly revealing deeper and deeper levels
of meaning.

The Zen canon contains the following story about the importance
of having humility whenever we listen to the Dharma:

A learned man once went to Zen Master Nan Yin and
asked him to explain Zen Buddhism to him. Master Nan
Yin placed a cup on a table and began pouring tea into it.
Then he continued to pour until the cup began to over-
flow.

The learned man said, 'Master, the cup already is
full.'

Master Nan Yin looked at the man and said, 'You are
just like this cup except you are full of concepts and

*ideas. If you want to learn Zen, you must first empty your
mind of all preconceptions."*

The benefits of listening to the Dharma

The *Saddharma Smriti Upasthana Sutra* mentions thirty-two benefits
that can be gained from listening to the Dharma. It says:

> *What are these thirty-two? When a master preaches the
> Dharma, he is like a parent to his audience, and he is
> like a bridge across the river of birth and death. When
> one hears what one has never heard before, one attains
> new realizations. Once one has knowledge, one can
> begin to think about what one has learned. Once one has
> begun to think about what one has learned, one has truly
> begun to practice self-cultivation. Once one has begun to
> practice self-cultivation, one will abide in peace. Once
> one has begun to abide in peace, one can begin to bene-
> fit others; and then a mutually beneficial interaction can
> begin. If one is able to abide in peace, then even hard-
> ship will not seem disturbing.*
>
> *If one listens to the Dharma, then roots of goodness
> will begin to grow where formerly they did not grow. If
> one contemplates what one has learned, then one will
> become prepared for liberation.*
>
> *Listening to the Dharma can lead people with
> perverse views to change their views to right ones and
> listening to the Dharma can help people destroy
> unwholesome thoughts whenever they arise. Listening to
> the Dharma increases goodness of mind and rids one of
> evil mental causes and conditions. Listening to the
> Dharma keeps one from being scattered and disorganized
> in one's activities. Listening to the Dharma leads one
> toward the company of good people and leads one away
> from selfishness and falseness. Listening to the Dharma
> encourages one to care for one's parents and believe in*

*karma; it also shows one how to live a long life.
Listening to the Dharma leads one to be praised by others and protected by heavenly beings, and it causes one's
deepest wishes to be fulfilled. Listening to the Dharma
brings one all the joys of the Dharma and keeps one from
sloth and laziness. Listening to the Dharma causes one to
progress quickly, to understand gratitude and to think
often on the meaning of death. If one has listened often
to the Dharma, at the time of one's death, one will not
cling to life or feel remorse for what one has done.
Ultimately, listening to the Dharma will lead one to
Nirvana.*

The right attitude for listening to the Dharma

It is important to have the right attitude when listening to the
Dharma. Whenever we are privileged to hear the Dharma we should
reflect on our good fortune as we strive to be respectful, receptive,
serious and thoughtful.

Master Yin Hsun suggests that we think of ourselves as patients
with a disease that only the Dharma can cure. In this respect, we
should consider the Buddha to be like a doctor and the Dharma to
be like a medicine. The Buddha gives us the right medicine, which
will cure us, but we ourselves must be sure to take the medicine. If
we do not, obviously it cannot possibly cure us.

When we listen to the Dharma, we must concentrate and we
must be careful not to allow fixed ideas to prevent the Buddha's mes-
sage from fully penetrating our minds. Our purpose in listening to
the Dharma must be to learn; if we think we already know what the
Buddha is going to say or if we think that we know more than the
Buddha, we will not be in the right frame of mind to benefit from his
teachings. Even after we believe we have really come to understand
some aspect of the Dharma, we must always keep our minds open so
that even higher levels of understanding can become available to us.
Short of full attainment of Buddhahood, there can be no end to the
learning process.

A human body is hard to attain,
but today we have one.
It is hard to get the chance
to hear the Dharma,
but today we have heard it.
If we do not practice in this life,
then in which life will we
finally begin?

— from the *Agamas*

Steady Progress

If you keep your practice steady,
morning and night, summer and winter,
there is nothing you cannot do
and nothing that can harm you.

— from the *Upasakashila Sutra*

The importance of being steady

Laziness and fear of work will get you into trouble no matter where they appear. Laziness is a basic animal tendency that must be confronted the moment it begins. Once you begin to allow yourself to be lazy, it will be hard for you to do anything successfully. Fear or dislike of work leads to a weak state of mind that tries to make quick profits or exploit the labor of others. You may get a leg up in the samsaric world once in a while by avoiding work, but eventually you will bring great harm to yourself. This world is the only place we have to practice Buddhism. If you are not practicing Buddhism all the time in everything that you do, you are not really practicing Buddhism, you are playing at it.

It is good sometimes to stress the arduousness of Buddhist practice. Having said that, let us remember as well that every gain made in understanding Buddhism pays back the effort put into it tenfold.

Buddhism is practiced at the point where the mind meets life; it is practiced in the mind as the mind is stimulated by life; and it is practiced in life where the mind learns everything it knows. We must not let ourselves become inattentive, dishonest, or lazy in our practice. There is much for all of us to learn, and not one of us will succeed without a steady application of energy to the task.

The *Sutra of Bequeathed Teachings* says,

> *If you make a steady effort to progress, you will find that nothing is too difficult. This is because steady effort is like running water; it can even cut through stones. Contrariwise, if you frequently abandon your effort to progress, you will go nowhere. You will be like someone who tries to start a fire by rubbing two sticks together but stops before the wood gets hot. You may desire to start a fire, but you will never succeed.*

The *Mahaprajnaparamita Shastra* says, "Steady progress is the source of all goodness. It gives birth to all good practice of the Dharma which ultimately leads to *anuttara-samyak-sambodhi* [the highest enlightenment]."

Steady progress is based on determination. The *Treatise on the Awakening of Faith in the Mahayana* says, "Generally speaking, there are three kinds of determination: determination born of faith, determination born of understanding and practice, and determination born of proven realization."

What is progress?

Progress in Buddhism is not something that can be judged or determined in samsaric terms. There is no equation between success in this world and progress in Buddhism. To progress quickly and with as few distractions as possible, a Buddhist should always look to what he is doing, not to what he is getting or how others are treating him.

The *Yogacharabhumi Shastra* recognizes five basic stages of progress in Buddhism:

1) The "shielded stage," during which the ambition to progress in Buddhism first appears. It is so called because the practitioner must be careful to protect himself from temptation and misunderstanding.

2) The "increased stage" during which the practitioner strengthens his resolve and begins to make vows.

3) The "stage of self-esteem" during which the practitioner becomes certain of the correctness of his path and does not fear what others may say about him.

4) The "independent stage" during which the practitioner is able to make steady progress no matter what circumstances he finds himself in.

5) The "stage of insufficiency" during which the practitioner realizes that he must give his whole heart to his practice and that anything less would be insufficient.

Progress can also be measured by consulting the Fifty-Two Stages of the Bodhi Way or the Thirty-Seven Conditions Leading to Buddhahood. See the *Agamas* for a good description of the Thirty-Seven Conditions or the *Avatamsaka Sutra* for a description of the Fifty-two Stages.

In the end, compassion is the most valuable measurement and guide for all Buddhist practice. Compassion is itself the highest awareness and the highest practice. If you feel any growth in compassion or toward compassion, you can be sure that you are progressing on the path toward enlightenment.

> *Taking no thought of the body*
> *and firm in wisdom and mind,*
> *steadily progressing in the Dharma,*
> *the practitioner will find that*
> *he achieves his goal and that*
> *nothing can obstruct him at all.*

— from the *Mahaprajnaparamita Shastra*

The Way to Practice

If your mind is in balance,
what need is there to work at morality?
If your behavior is correct,
what use is meditation to you?
If you understand mercy,
then you will naturally care for your parents.
If you understand faithful conduct,
then all of society will be in order.

— from the *Platform Sutra of the Sixth Patriarch*

A balanced mind

Mental balance results from understanding that self-respect is a natural outgrowth of having respect for others. If we know how to respect others, then we will know how to respect ourselves. If we know how to respect ourselves, then we will seldom feel anxious or moody; our minds will be in balance and our practice of morality will seem effortless. This is why Hui Neng made the above remarks in the *Platform Sutra of the Sixth Patriarch*.

Another reason he made the above remarks is he wanted to help us free ourselves from having an oppressive sense of morality or moral duty. Many people believe that a moral lifestyle must be confining or stifling, because they can conceive of it only as a serious abridgment of their freedom. To people of this type, agreeing to be moral feels like signing an unwanted contract.

Nothing could be further from the truth. Morality is the only way to make yourself truly free. When you understand this, you will realize that the moral injunctions taught by the Buddha are keys to our liberation. These keys do not lock us into a narrow prison cell; they free us from a narrow cell. Once one has been freed from the bonds of delusion, one achieves a mental balance that almost makes the observance of morality unnecessary.

Correct behavior

The purpose of meditation is to settle the mind and allow it to look directly at itself. A deluded and egocentric mind may benefit somewhat from meditation, but no one can make real progress in understanding the mind through meditation unless they simultaneously begin bringing their behavior into accord with Buddhist morality.

Hui Neng said, "If your behavior is correct, what use is meditation to you?" He said this to emphasize the importance of morality, not to downplay the importance of meditation. Hui Neng was one of the greatest Zen masters who ever lived. In this statement, like the one before it, he is trying to free us from feeling that our practice must be difficult or oppressive, or that it has no further goal than itself. Once our minds have achieved balance, morality will flow naturally, almost effortlessly. And once we have learned to behave well in all circumstances, our lives will be in accord with the deepest levels of meditation.

How we actually treat other people is the best standard we have to judge ourselves. How they treat us, what we are getting from the world, the depth of our meditation—these are secondary.

Mercy

"If you understand mercy, then you will naturally care for your parents." Hui Neng used the word mercy (*en*) in this verse. This word can also be translated into English as grace or kindness. *En*, or mercy, is close in meaning to the word compassion. *En*, however, contains the idea that one should repay whatever mercy or kindness one has received from others. In Chinese, "to feel *en*" toward someone means to be grateful to them for something they have done for us.

In this line, Hui Neng is saying that once one's sense of gratitude is developed, one naturally will be inclined to respect and care for one's parents as well as all other sentient beings.

This verse does not mean that we should expect to profit from acts of kindness toward others. It only means that we should all deeply appreciate how much others have done for us. Appreciation of others is a fundamental starting point for the successful practice of Buddhism.

Faithful conduct

"If you understand faithful conduct, then all of society will be in order."

"Faithful conduct" here means right conduct, right action, right view. If all of us were to follow the Noble Eightfold Path, then society would be in order.

In these verses, Hui Neng has asked us to turn our awareness inward and concentrate on the sources of our consciousness and behavior. This is the fundamental work of Buddhist practice. All the methods of Buddhism come down to nothing much more than this. When we see ourselves as we really are, we see the truth. We see the Buddha within.

> Master P'u Ming asked, "What is Buddha nature?"
> Master Hsing Sze replied, "You have no Buddha nature."
> Master P'u Ming said, "All creatures including insects have Buddha nature. Why do you say that I do not have one?"
> Master Hsing Sze replied, "Because you are looking for it outside of yourself."
> Master P'u Ming said, "Then how do I find it?"
> Master Hsing Sze said, "You will not find it by covering it up."
> Master P'u Ming said, "Then how do I find it?"
> Master Hsing Sze said, "By giving it up."

> — from the Zen canon

Beneficial Practice

*The wise who live in this world
often perform beneficial deeds.
To come to understand yourself
is the most beneficial deed of all.*

— from the *Dharmapada*

The wise who live in this world

This *saha* world is built out of the interplay of paired opposites, and thus it appears to us to be made of halves: half dark, half light, half good, half bad, half wise and half ignorant.

A person who is wise will do his best to bring happiness to those around him. He will work to infuse positive energy into his world and he will be a source of higher awareness whenever he can. In contrast, an ignorant person always wants to do the opposite; he is negative, mean-spirited, and quick to take delight when things go wrong. Rather than help others, he always wants to hinder them and drag them down to his own low level.

Most people are mixtures of the kinds of energies described above. Once this is understood, one will naturally begin to want to be wiser rather than more ignorant. The greatest wisdom in Buddhism is prajna wisdom: the wisdom that understands the underlying emptiness of all phenomena, while at the same time, understanding the need for compassion. One who possesses prajna wisdom is able to overcome all difficulties. Prajna wisdom leads quickly to enlightenment because it cannot be mired in samsaric duality or in attachment to any illusion.

Often perform beneficial deeds

How is one to attain prajna wisdom?

The Buddhist sutras tell us there are two basic ways:

1) The first way is the way of the "three studies." These are the study of the precepts of Buddhism, the study of meditation, and the study of the principles of Buddhism.

2) The second way is the way of regularly listening to the Dharma. It is very important to listen often to the Dharma. If someone near you is going to speak on the Dharma, by all means go and listen. Take time to discuss the Dharma with your friends. Think about it, read books about it, study the sutras. Our whole purpose for studying Buddhism is to grow toward higher awareness. Studying the Dharma will result in personal growth. This is why it is so important to keep studying; as we learn and grow, our comprehension of the Dharma will actually change. The Dharma never is the same to the same person at different times because the same person at different times never is the same. One of the most beautiful things about the Dharma is its capacity to yield higher and higher interpretations as our studies progress.

If we are actively reaching out to others and daily reflecting on the Dharma, we can be sure that we are often "performing beneficial deeds," deeds which benefit both self and others at the same time.

To come to understand yourself

Since the entire cosmos is contained in mind, understanding the mind is the ultimate goal of all truth-seekers. Constant effort must be applied to the task. This means that we practice Buddhism all day long every day, wherever we are. This is humanistic Buddhism. Our minds are stimulated and challenged by other people more than by anything else. Once we recognize this, we will realize that to practice Buddhism apart from other people is to turn away from the very essence of ourselves and of Buddhism. Buddhism is a religion founded on human nature. You will come to understand yourself, ultimately, only through your interactions with other people.

The most basic kinds of wisdom are called the Wisdom Gates. The first Wisdom Gate is the gate which leads to enlightenment of the self. The second Wisdom Gate is the gate which leads to compassion for all other sentient beings.

The wisdom of a Buddha can be described as being perfect, being pure, knowing all things, having limitless compassion and perfect skill to teach others. The *Yogacarabhumi Sastra* says, "Perfect wisdom (*sarvajna*) is never obstructed by anything in any realm, by any event or phenomena, by any thing, or by any time."

To achieve enlightenment in the bodhi mind, a bodhisattva must practice the Six Paramitas. Among them is *prajna paramita*, or the Paramita of Great Wisdom. This *paramita* is sometimes called "the Mother of all Buddhas" because it is essential to the practice of Buddhism.

Prajna wisdom is of two kinds: common wisdom, which is available to all Buddhists, and uncommon wisdom, which is only realized by the bodhisattva. Uncommon wisdom is the understanding that Buddhism cannot ultimately be practiced for the self alone; it must be shared with others.

Another way of understanding prajna wisdom is to understand that it is comprised of "the wisdom of this world" and "the wisdom which transcends this world." The life of the bodhisattva is based on transcendental wisdom and goals, and it is fully informed by both of them. At the same time, however, the bodhisattva does not abandon this world. He lives in it fully and gives the best of himself at all times.

The most beneficial deed of all

To fully achieve prajna wisdom means to realize that the universe is bigger than you are. It is bigger than you and it is you. It is in your head and it transcends everything in your head. Prajna wisdom pervades the entire expanse. There is nothing which escapes its concern or is beneath its concern. There is nothing which is not an intimate part of it. When a practitioner realizes this simple yet overwhelming truth, he or she will immediately begin to bring enormous benefit to all other sentient beings in the universe. Ships in the sea rise together. Birds learn the air by watching other birds.

The Buddha said: To be generous
without the Paramita of Great Wisdom
will not help anyone cross to the other shore.
If you want to cross to the other shore,
you must base your generosity on the
Paramita of Great Wisdom.
And all of the other paramitas are the same:
discipline, patience, progress, contemplation;
all of them must be based on the
. Paramita of Great Wisdom.
Why is this so?
This is so because the
Paramita of Great Wisdom alone
sees the fundamental equality of all things.

— from the *Mahaprajnaparamita Sutra*

Sickness

We should look after those who are ill
and inquire about their troubles.
You will reap what you sow;
your fields will grow
what you have planted in them.

— from the *Jatakanidana*

The inevitability of illness

The first Noble Truth of Buddhism states that life is unsatisfactory.
A large part of this truth rests on the fact that no one can escape
sickness, old age, and death. The certainty of illness causes suffering
and yet it also stimulates us to seek liberation in the Dharma. In this
samsaric world good can be seen in the bad and bad can be seen in
the good; everything is mixed. If we look always toward the bad, our
eyes will fill with darkness and fear. If we look often toward the good,
however, we will gradually begin to elevate ourselves above the claws
of duality.

Sickness is one of the Eight Sufferings. Sickness follows health
and health follows sickness. We all must be prepared to die. The
decline of the physical form is inevitable. While we are healthy, therefore, it is important that we use our time in such a way that we bring
maximum benefit to others. Appreciation of the inevitability of sickness is an excellent stimulant of compassion. We only have a little

time to grow and express ourselves. Cherish your time with others; encourage them; be a positive influence on them if you can.

The *Jatakanidana* says, "Of all forms of suffering, illness is the worst. Of all good deeds, helping the ill is the best."

It is important to help people who are ill, because when we become ill our bodies are weakened and this leads to a decline of willpower or inner resolve. People who are ill are more prone than others to depression, anxiety, and other forms of emotional tribulation. These are the times when people are most in need of other people. They need our encouragement, our warmth, and our kindness more than at any other time.

How to care for the ill

Not only will all of us experience illness in this life, but all of us also will be in a position at some time in our lives to help someone else who is ill. There is a natural tendency sometimes to want to turn away from people who are ill. This tendency, for the most part, is born of ignorance of what to do for them. When we are in a position to care for someone who is ill, it is important that we act wisely. If we ourselves are confused about what we are doing, we may bring more harm than good to the situation.

The *Ekottarika Agama* mentions five important points on which we should base our care of the ill:

1) Be sure the person is seeing a competent doctor. Once we are under the care of a physician, it is important to trust him. However, we must all also take some responsibility ourselves. In the case of serious illness, it is always a good idea to get a second opinion on treatment.

2) Do not become lazy or inattentive. Your attitude toward what you are doing will be transmitted to the person who is ill. Get up early, keep their room and clothing clean, straighten the bed and be sure the person is as comfortable as can be.

3) Speak positively. Speak often to the person who is ill, using words of praise and encouragement whenever possible. Your speech can help them overcome loneliness and depression as it bolsters

them with sociable and life-giving feelings. Don't shut them away and pretend they no longer are part of the world or that their opinions no longer matter. When people feel involved in the events around them, they get well much more quickly.

4) Don't sleep too much or ignore the person who is ill. You should be attentive to their needs and sensitive to the fact that they may have needs that are difficult for them to express. Flowers, sunshine, artwork, or the right kind of reading material can do wonders for someone who is ill. The fact that others are paying attention to them is a great source of comfort to anyone who is not feeling well.

5) Speak about the Dharma. Keep the precepts while you are around the ill person and provide them with Buddhist materials if these seem helpful. People who are ill should be reminded that everything, including illness, is transitory. In the highest levels of reality, there is no such thing as illness.

If these five points are closely followed, good health will usually quickly return.

The rewards of caring for the ill

All acts of sincere generosity produce good rewards. The *Mahaparinirvana Sutra* says, "Being generous toward the ill and caring for the ill is one of the greatest forms of generosity."

The *Brahmajala Sutra* says, "If any Buddhist should make offerings to an ill person or care for an ill person as if they were no different from the Buddha himself, then they will have planted great good seeds in the best of the eight fields of good reward."

From many other places in the sutras, we can see that Buddha considered care of the ill to be very important. He said many times that caring for the ill would lead to good rewards in the future.

The sutras also mention many occasions when the Buddha himself cared for disciples who were ill: he washed them, washed their clothes, swept the floor, and used encouraging language so that they would feel well cared for and well appreciated. Part of the greatness of the Buddha was his capacity to remember the importance of the small things in life, even as he was able to see beyond this world completely. His mind was able to penetrate the deepest truths of the universe and yet at the same time he was also able to sweep the floor and mend clothing.

The great Chinese translator of Buddhist sutras, Hsuan Tsang, similarly, did not feel he was above helping others. Before he left for India on his great journey to collect Buddhist sutras, Hsuan Tsang cared for a dirty and lowly monk until he was cured. As Hsuan Tsang watched over him, the monk taught him the shorter *Prajnaparamita Sutra*. Many years later, Hsuan Tsang produced the finest translation ever made in Chinese of the long version of this sutra. Hsuan Tsang's *Mahaprajnaparamita Sutra* is still the standard version of this sutra used today in China.

The sages of old used to say, "One seed of grain planted in the spring produces ten thousand seeds in the autumn. Good and bad behavior both bring certain results."

They also used to say, "If you plant a melon seed, you will get a melon. If you plant a bean, you will get a bean."

Conclusion

There is another old saying: "A flower's redness lasts less than one hundred days. In this life a human being has fewer than one thousand good days."

While we are healthy we should use our time well. We should fill our lives with wholesome, positive activity and never shirk the duty to care for ailing friends or relatives. Good behavior is good in and of itself, but it is also a means to improve ourselves as we gradually better our own conditions by planting seeds of compassion and kindness in the world around us.

When people near to you fall ill, don't wait for them to ask for your help. This is the time to reach out and be generous with your life. Your caring kindness will go a long way toward improving this world.

> *Life and death flicker like flames.*
> *Suffering goes on and on.*
> *Take the Mahayana vow*

to save all sentient ones.
Vow to stand in for them
and carry their burdens for them.
Vow to lead them all
to the shores of ultimate joy.

— from the *Eight Realizations of the Bodhisattva Sutra*

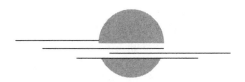

How to Manage Wealth

When you begin in a trade or profession,
it is appropriate to accumulate wealth.
Once you have accumulated some wealth,
you should divide it into four parts:
one part to be used for daily necessities,
two parts to be used for your profession,
one part to be saved in case of unexpected need.

— from the *Samyukta Agama*

Appropriate ways to gain wealth
Buddhism has never been a religion that rejects wealth. Some of the most important early Buddhists were wealthy kings or wealthy merchants. Without their help, it is doubtful whether Buddhism would have spread as far as it did as quickly as it did.

Wealth can be like a poisonous snake if it is acquired illegally or if it inspires the mind to become lustful or greedy. At the same time, legally acquired wealth in the hands of a wise and generous person can bring great benefit to the world. Donations from wealthy people are a major source of funds needed to spread the Dharma, to publish Dharma literature, and to build temples. The heart of Buddhist morality is intention. If our intentions are good, we will be able to use wealth to benefit others. If our intentions are not good, we will be a negative influence in the world whether we are wealthy or poor .

How to acquire wealth

The most basic way to acquire wealth is to learn a skill. Once one has acquired a skill, then one must practice it with diligence and complete honesty. The money one earns through the practice of one's profession should be saved, invested and used wisely. If one consumes too much or if one develops too many expensive habits, then one's wealth will only become an agent of harm. Money should never be used to harm anyone.

The Buddha specifically mentioned several ways that one must not acquire wealth. Whether these ways are legal in your country or not, the Buddha stated specifically that one must not operate or work in a gambling establishment, a place which serves drugs or alcohol, a slaughterhouse or in the hunting or fishing industries.

The *Sigalovada Sutra* says:

> Anyone who wants to acquire wealth must know that
> there are six ways of gaining wealth which run contrary
> to Buddhist morality. These six ways are: 1) devious or
> tricky ways, 2) ill-timed ways, 3) sloppy ways or ways
> which use alcoholic beverages, 4) ways which depend on
> evil companions, 5) ways which depend on prostitution,
> and 6) lazy and slothful ways.

How to use wealth

The Buddha spoke fairly often on the subject of how one should use material wealth. In the *Samyukta Agama,* he suggested the four divisions of wealth quoted at the beginning of this section. In the *Maharatnakuta Sutra,* the Buddha tells the wealthy King Prasenajit that he should think of his wealth as being divided into three parts. The Buddha suggested that one part be used for the encouragement of religion, one part for helping the poor and one part for national investments. In the *Mahaparinirvana Sutra,* the Buddha suggested another four-part plan for our wealth. He said that one part should be used for taking care of our parents and immediate family members, one part should be used for helping employees or others who

are dependent on us, one part should be given to friends and relatives, and one part should be given to the monastic community.
The Buddha was a practical and skillful thinker. He taught his followers how to achieve control over all aspects of their lives. Since the society to which the Buddha spoke was so much different from the ones we live in today, it is important for all of us to extract the core spirit of his words and not attach ourselves to exact divisions mentioned long ago. The Buddha often said different things to different groups of people at different places. This was how he taught. These were his skillful means. A wealthy person can actually consider giving one fourth of his wealth to a monastery, while a poor person cannot.

The heart of the Buddha's teachings on wealth is to acquire it honestly and use it to help others. Wealth gives us a material opportunity to practice the positive aspects of Buddhist morality in this world; through the thoughtful and generous use of wealth we can learn non-attachment, compassion, generosity, and clear thinking. In the end, the greatest wealth of all is knowledge of our own Buddha nature. One glimpse of the awesome spiritual wealth that lies within you is worth more than all of the material wealth in the universe.

Subhuti, if a bodhisattva is
attached to his own generosity,
then when he is generous
he will be like one who enters
a dark room and sees nothing.

If a bodhisattva is not attached
to his own generosity,
then when he is generous
he will be like one standing
in the sunlight and he will see
all colors and forms clearly.

— from the *Diamond Sutra*

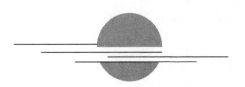

Generosity

You may intend to cause benefit
through offerings made to evil people,
but you will only cause more harm;
making such offerings is like
feeding a savage beast;
everyone is hurt by the deed.

— from the *Sutra on the Principles of the Six Paramitas*

Merit gained from helping the virtuous

In Buddhist sutras, generosity is often compared to farming; if a farmer's fields are fertile, his harvest will be large and good. It is much the same with people; if you plant your generosity in the right place, you will receive great benefit. If you are generous toward virtuous people, then both you and others will benefit greatly from your action.

This is why the *Sutra in Forty-Two Sections* says, "Feeding a hundred evil people is not as good as feeding one good person. Feeding a thousand good people is not as good as feeding one who upholds the precepts. Feeding ten thousand people who uphold the precepts is not as good as feeding one *shrotapanna*. Feeding one million *shrotapanna* is not as good as feeding one *sakadagami*. Feeding ten million Sakadagami is not as good as feeding one *anagami*. Feeding one hundred million *anagami* is not as good as feeding one *arhat*. Feeding one billion *arhats* is not as good as feeding one *pratyeka-buddha*.

Feeding ten billion *pratyeka-buddhas* is not as good as feeding one Buddha of the past, present and future."

To whom should we be generous?

Buddhist sutras mention three kinds of people to whom we should be generous:

1) People who are suffering. We should expend great effort in trying to help those who are suffering.

2) People who have been kind to us. We should repay in abundance the kindness shown to us by our parents, our teachers and our elders.

3) The Buddha, the Dharma, and the Sangha. All offerings and all respect shown toward the Triple Gem will bring unlimited merit and benefit to all of us.

How to be generous toward wrong-doers

Clearly we should not completely abandon people who have done wrong, but we must think carefully about how we are going to help them once we have determined that our help is needed. If we are not careful about how we decide to help them, our generosity may end up causing more harm than good. When we help someone, we must be sure that our help does not become a means for that person to bring even more trouble on himself and others.

People do wrong out of greed, ignorance, or anger. These three defilements are the root causes of all problems in the world. When we seek for ways to help someone who has acted from the promptings of one of these three defilements, we must be sure that our help will lead the person in question toward a deeper understanding of the cause of his transgression. If our "help" only humiliates him or makes him angry, we will not have succeeded in being truly generous. If our "help" only smoothes over deeper problems and allows the wrong-doer to continue in his ways without correcting them, then our generosity may ultimately become the cause of a third person's suffering.

The fact that it is difficult to offer aid that will truly benefit others does not mean that we should not try. If our intentions are pure, there will be good results in the end. For the most part, true generosity should lead the wrong-doer toward greater wisdom and understanding.

> *Everything has its time.*
> *If the time is not right but still*
> *you force your will on events,*
> *then you will bring trouble to yourself.*
> *For this reason it is said that*
> *everyone should know the difference between*
> *the right time and the wrong time.*

> — from the *Sutra of One Hundred Parables*

How to be generous toward children

Generosity should never produce or encourage sloth, depravity, insensitivity, irresponsibility or meanness. If parents are lax with their children under the guise of being generous with them, they will only bring harm to themselves, their children and society. There is a fine but very important line between discipline and affection, between what is good for our children and what harms them. Children who are given lots of money but not directed in how to use it too often lose touch with other people. Since their emotions have been nurtured in a protective and unnatural environment, they misunderstand the needs and feelings of others and bring harm both to themselves and to those who are around them.

Ideally, generosity directed toward children should nurture their higher moral qualities. Generosity should teach children how to be unattached to material things and how to place the well-being of others above their own.

The three kinds of generosity

Generosity properly is an aspect of compassion. Since true compassion seeks only the well-being of others, all acts of generosity should be directed toward increasing the well-being of others. Buddhist sutras speak of three basic kinds of generosity:

1) Material generosity. By giving things to others we give them joy and comfort. In the highest sense, our generosity should be a gift of kindness that nurtures the moral nature of others as it shows them, very simply, that we care about them.

2) Emotional generosity. When we are generous with our time and our emotions, we help others overcome the hardships of life. Our laughter will help them endure, our kindness will keep them from fear, while our sensitivity will help them realize the oneness of all sentient beings.

3) Dharma generosity. In the end, the highest form of generosity is giving the Dharma. Only the Dharma can give others the means to stand on their own and truly understand life in this world. Whenever we speak about the Dharma, or teach it or encourage others in it, we are giving the highest gift of all.

> *When a bodhisattva is generous,*
> *he contemplates that the giver, the gift*
> *and the recipient of the gift*
> *are completely empty.*
> *His contemplations*
> *carry him beyond all obstructions,*
> *all greed and all defilement.*
> *This is what is called the*
> *"Accomplished Generosity" of the bodhisattva.*

— from the *Rain of Treasures Sutra*

Not Killing

All beings fear death
and they all fear the pain of a club.
Think: how do they make you feel?
Then do not kill and do not club;
live peacefully with all beings and
do not add to the violence of this world.
Harm no one here
and you will pass your next life in peace.

— from the *Dharmapada*

Why we should not kill

Life is more precious than anything else in the world. Even insects want to live. Whenever we break any of the Five Precepts of Buddhism, we have violated some other sentient being. Whenever we kill anything, we violate that being at the deepest level possible. Killing, thus, is an action that must be avoided by all Buddhists.

Some killing is undertaken senselessly. Children sometimes kill small creatures without giving any thought to their deeds. This kind of killing is based on ignorance of the oneness of all of life. Children should be taught that their actions are depriving an essential part of themselves from having vital freedom. When this kind of killing persists into adulthood, it is a sign that the person in question is lacking in higher wisdom. The actions of an adult are far more intentional than those of a child, and thus adults ultimately will reap far more karmic retribution for their deeds than a child. The *Mahaprajnaparamita Shastra* says:

> If one should decide to kill a sentient being while know-
> ing full well that that being is a sentient being, then one
> will create karma of the body and defile one's inner
> moral nature. Karma of the body and defilement of one's
> inner moral nature comprise the two aspects of what is
> called the transgression of killing. Beyond this, shackling
> people or confining them to small spaces, whipping them
> or beating them are forms of torture that are almost as
> bad as killing. When one kills another outright, one has
> committed the transgression of killing. When one
> appoints someone else to kill in one's stead, if one knows
> full well that the being being killed is a sentient being,
> then one also has committed the transgression of killing.
>
> One cannot pretend that one does not know what
> one is doing if one does. Excuses are useless. If one sees a
> person at night and says that he is just a tree stump and
> then kills him, one still has killed no matter what the
> excuse; and one still has committed the transgression of
> killing.
>
> If one kills out of passion, one cannot use the excuse
> of insanity or stupidity; one has still committed the trans-
> gression of killing.
>
> If one destroys the life of another, one cannot say that
> one has simply removed a boil; one has still committed
> the transgression of killing.
>
> Killing results in karmic retribution. If one orders
> someone else to kill someone, one still has committed the
> transgression of killing. The karmic retribution for hav-
> ing given the order to kill will not be confined to retribu-
> tion for bad speech alone.
>
> All of these kinds of killing are killing plain and
> simple.

> *If you do not do any of these kinds of killing then you*
> *are keeping the precept of not killing.*
>
> *Anyone who takes this precept to heart and vows,*
> *"From this day on I will never kill again"—that person is*
> *keeping the precept of not killing.*
>
> *And if this person keeps this vow in body and speech,*
> *if he promises, "I will never kill again," then he is keep-*
> *ing the precept of not killing.*

The rewards of not killing

Vowing not to kill, and upholding that vow, brings many rewards. As with all the precepts of Buddhism, one gains far more than one loses by choosing to live a morally proper life.

Consciously and consistently refraining from killing increases one's sensitivity to the needs and feelings of all sentient beings as it helps one to understand that all appearances of separation between sentient beings are illusions. Compassion, sensitivity, and the vow not to kill are very deep aspects of the understanding that all of life is one.

When one kills, one's mind is always full of poisons. When one does not kill, the mind is free and light.

When one kills, one increases negativity and anger in oneself and in the world. When one does not kill, one increases positive and joyful emotions in oneself and the world.

When one kills, one is always anxious and cannot sleep. When one does not kill, one begins to learn that truly there is nothing anywhere to fear and that all is joy.

When one kills, one will be terrified at the time of one's own death and one will not obtain a good rebirth. When one does not kill, one will obtain a good rebirth in circumstances that will lead quickly toward enlightenment.

> *Because there is transgression,*
> *there is birth.*
> *Because there is birth,*
> *there is death.*

*Birth and death
arise from transgression.
When all transgressions
have completely ceased,
then there is wisdom.*

—from the *Shurangama Sutra*

Not Lying

> *Deceit is the source of all evil.*
> *It destroys good practice.*
> *It brings harm to others and*
> *nothing good can be said about it.*

—from the *Suratapariprccha Sutra*

Trustworthy words

If you lie, you will not be trusted. If you cannot be trusted, you will be ineffective in your own life and useless to other people. Lies hurt others because they damage their trust and their sense of what is right and wrong. This is a very serious kind of damage; it wastes time, frightens people, and causes them to doubt their basic intuitions and feelings. It is a deep violation of another person to lie to them. Whenever we violate another, we also violate ourselves. On top of that, our own lies hurt us terribly because they force us to waste energy maintaining an illusion that we know is not true. This waste of energy greatly decreases our capacity to function effectively in this world and it greatly lessens our ability to absorb the truths of Buddhism.

The *Questions of the Precious Girl Sutra* says, "The bodhisattva has three basic practices that he must work on until they are perfected: he must never lie to the Buddha, he must never lie to himself and he must never lie to anyone else."

The harm caused by lying
Lying has many names. Some of them are deceit, duplicity, slander, distortion, fabrication, fraud, misrepresentation, falsification, forgery, perjury. These are all generally recognized as being criminal acts, but lying can also be conducted under the banner of lofty ideals. This kind of lying is called hypocrisy. The Buddha said that lying is one of the ten evil deeds. Its purpose is to deceive others in order to get something from them, to prevent them from getting something, or to harm them.

Lies are serious offenses and one lie usually leads to another and then another. It does not take much thought to realize how great a burden a bundle of lies can be. They are hard to carry and they weigh us down a lot. They bring harm to everyone involved and they never produce good results in the long run. Sentient beings generate much of their bad karma and attachment to samsara through lying alone.

The *Saddharma Smirti Upasthana Sutra* says:

> One who lies brings trouble to all sentient beings. A lie
> is like a blanket of darkness or like death among the
> living. To tell a lie is like cutting your own tongue with
> a knife; how can this not bring you harm? To lie is to
> disgrace yourself; it is like carrying a poisonous snake in
> your mouth; it is like carrying a knife in your mouth; it
> is like carrying a burning fire in your mouth. The poison
> of a poisonous snake is bad, but it is not nearly as bad as
> the poison of a lying mouth because a lie hurts all
> sentient beings and eventually leads the liar himself to
> descend into the hell realms. When a person lies, it is as
> if pus were dripping from his mouth; his tongue becomes
> mucked up and filthy and it burns with a terrible heat.
> Lies are like shackles which bind us. They destroy the
> bridge of the Dharma.

In its "Hell" chapter, the *Saddharma Smirti Upasthana Sutra* says:

> Don't lie! Lies produce all manner of evil and lead to
> continuous entrapment in the cycle of birth and death.

> *Lies obscure the good and conceal what is right and they*
> *lead to a bad rebirth and an ugly appearance. Lies lead*
> *to loss and vacancy. When a person lies, it is as if he cuts*
> *off his own tongue with an ax. Lies are the banners of*
> *evil and they bind us to evil places. They are the sources*
> *of ignorance and darkness.*

The karmic results of lying

According to the *Mahaprajnaparamita Shastra*, lying without regret or repentance will completely block the way to enlightenment and bring the following ten unhappy results: bad breath, a loss of protection by good spirits and a gaining of trouble caused by evil spirits, not being trusted by others even if what one says is true, not being included in the company of the wise, often being slandered and insulted, not being respected by others, having frequent feelings of anxiety, planting the seeds of ill-repute, rebirth in hell, often being slandered.

A lie works against the flow of truth and compassion; how could it lead anywhere but to problems and suffering?

The importance of using language to good effect

Truth is powerful. In the moment it may seem to be more difficult to tell the truth than to lie, but in the long run truth is always the better option. Nothing good can come from bad motives and nothing good can come of lies. The wise never lie because they can see the consequences.

In some ways, we should almost feel grateful that lying exists in this world because it is generally easier to see the results of breaking the precepts by lying than it is by the other basic transgressions. Analyze yourself; analyze any lie you may ever have spoken. Isn't the twisting and turning of the mind as it tries and tries to justify itself an obvious burden that becomes much worse than simply telling the truth in the first place?

When we don't lie, we begin to use language well. A confidence and certainty enters the tone of voice as our ability to express ourselves improves. Language is most beautiful when it is true.

Compassion is most perfect when it is sincere. When we are honest, our speech and our attitudes toward life reveal levels of profundity and commitment that transcend the samsaric flux of ordinary existence.

Remember, our original teacher, the Buddha, is known as "the one of truthful words, the one of real words, the one whose words are thus, the one who never lies." Because of these qualities, the Buddha was able to establish the Dharma in this world for the purpose of leading sentient beings toward enlightenment. Those of us who follow the Buddha today should never forget the primary virtue of always telling the truth.

> *The light of my wisdom*
> *shines without ending.*
> *The length of my life*
> *goes on and on.*
> *These are the results of*
> *constant cultivation.*
> *Those of you who are wise*
> *should doubt none of this*
> *for the words of a Buddha*
> *are true and never false.*

> — from the *Lotus Sutra*

Patience Under Insult

Where does the greatest power lie?
It lies in patience under insult.
Those who are patient do not feel resentment
and thus they are honored by all.

— from the *Sutra in Forty-Two Sections*

The power of patience

The patience we are discussing here is that kind of patience which is able to endure hardship, disgrace, calamity, and bad luck. This kind of patience can triumph over anything. Remember, everything is transient. Nothing lasts forever. When we approach hardship with an attitude of acceptance and patience, we already have gone a long way toward improving our situation. What we resist persists. Patience should be our first response. When we allow our lives to be guided by patience and humility, we cannot go wrong.

The *Patience of Rahula Sutra* says:

> *Patience is clear and bright like sunlight or moonlight.*
> *The dragon and elephant are very strong, but even together*
> *they do not have a thousandth part of the strength of one*
> *who is patient. Common people believe jewels and*
> *treasures are the greatest things. They do not see the*
> *calamities they cause and the pain. The real, true treasure*
> *is patience, for it always assures one of peace and it always*
> *treats others well and it always brings the greatest reward.*

The *Dharmapada* says, "The best way to rid yourself of anger is through patience."

The importance of patience

In this section we are mainly discussing "patience under insult" or "patience under disgrace" because insult and disgrace are the most difficult assaults most of us ever have to endure. Since we all are social beings, we all feel the sting of disgrace or the slap of insult more sharply than anything else. Hunger, fatigue, hard work, even illness and loss are generally easier for most people to bear than ridicule, disgrace, or insult.

The Buddha was very wise and that is why he went straight to the heart of the matter in his discussions of patience. Being patient can be compared to accepting a burden, to recognizing a truth, to managing something, to sacrificing something, to making a resolution, to being courageous, to being fearless or to being wise.

Each of us will understand patience in our own way. This is because none of us needs to be patient, except insofar as we have a false sense of self that feels the need to endure something it doesn't like. Saints have no need of patience. Advanced practitioners enjoy insults since they provide an excellent chance to learn and improve. Some people want to fight when they are insulted. Others want to cry. Others want to justify themselves. The responses are many. The cause is but one—the illusion of self has been stimulated to defend itself against a well-aimed attack. The cure is to understand that there is nothing to be attacked and there is no attack; both of them are empty.

You cannot feel insulted unless you are deluded. All anger is an illusion. To understand this is to understand the highest form of patience. At its highest level, patience is just another word for wisdom.

The *Upasakashila Sutra* says:

> There are two kinds of patience: the patience of this
> world and the patience which transcends this world.
> In the patience of this world, we learn to endure
> hunger, thirst, heat, cold, suffering, and joy.

> *In the patience which transcends this world we learn*
> *to be steady in belief, wisdom, generosity, compassion and*
> *open-mindedness. We learn to be steadfast in our loyalty*
> *to the Buddha, Dharma, and Sangha and we learn to*
> *endure insults, beatings, taunting, evil plots against us,*
> *greed, anger, ignorance and all the other vile and humili-*
> *ating things of this world. We learn to endure the unen-*
> *durable and to accomplish the impossible. This is what is*
> *known as the patience which transcends this world.*

There are four basic ways to face situations that may call for our patience: 1) When you are insulted, do not respond. Silence is the best answer. 2) If you are to be beaten, become peaceful in your own mind. A peaceful mind can endure anything and it will always prevail in the end. 3) When you must take the brunt of someone's jealous hatred, return it with compassion. In the end, even a flicker of compassion can melt all the hatred in the world. 4) When you are slandered and insulted, contemplate virtue and mercy. The sting of insult makes virtue grow, while the absurdity of slander informs the mind of the importance of mercy.

How to be patient under insult and disgrace

The *Yogacharabhumi Shastra* says that true patience under insult requires that we not become angry, that we not become resentful and that we not harbor evil thoughts.

Master Han Shan said, "If you want to follow the bodhisattva path, protect your true mind with patience under insult."

In the *Sutra of Bequeathed Teachings*, the Buddha said, "Those who are able to be patient become powerful and great."

True patience requires no energy. If you have to expend energy to be patient, you can be sure your patience will not last. Patience is found in resting in the spaces between thoughts. Patience is calm and nonjudgmental. It is humble and wise in that it does not expect to be first or to have everything go its own way all the time.

If you find yourself losing your patience, first, watch what you say. Be patient with speech. Don't say something nasty. Second, be careful about your facial expression and your body language. Don't express disapproval through your posture or attitude. Third, observe your mind. Untoward emotions in their basic states are nothing but surges of energy. If we do not label them as anger or impatience, we will find that they are valuable sources of energy. Fourth, remember that karma and conditions produce the appearance of a world around us. If we do not accept our conditions, we will not learn from them. If we do not learn from them, they will not change.

The benefits of patience

Patience brings many benefits. Patience teaches us and helps us grow quickly and efficiently toward full realization of the indwelling Buddha mind.

The four most basic benefits conferred by patience are:

1) Patience dissipates anger. The *Avadanas* say, "You must not repay anger with anger for anger must come to an end. By being patient you will bring an end to anger; this is the way of the Tathagata."

Patience exhausts more than just the anger the person who is being patient might feel. Patience exhausts the anger of all who are around it because it gives that anger nothing to feed on. Without fuel, anger cannot burn for long.

2) Patience is a reliable refuge. In this world of suffering and pain, patience is our only certain refuge. The *Patience of Rahula Sutra* says:

> There is no refuge in this world except reliance on
> patience. Patience is a peaceful dwelling where disasters
> cannot begin. Patience is an armor which a band of sol-
> diers can not penetrate. Patience is a raft which will
> carry us across troubled waters. Patience is a medicine
> which can save our lives. The determination of one who
> is patient is strong enough to keep any vow.

3) Patience is the source of great goodness. It is a hidden virtue. It may not always obvious to others, but it always produces much goodness. The *Mahasamnipata* says that patience is the highest virtue and the way to peace and happiness. It says that patience leads one out of isolation while providing one with the joys of a sage. The

Mahasamnipata continues with a long list of the benefits of practicing patience. It says that patience can be a friend, that it can improve your reputation, that it is loved by all the world, that it is a benefit in and of itself, that it is magnificent, that it brings one great power, that its light shines over the world, that it achieves all happiness, that it creates success, that it defeats anger, that it eradicates suffering, that it produces a pleasant appearance, that it provides a good family, that it receives many rewards, that it is the best path, that it brings joy to people, that it achieves many wonderful things, that it removes all trouble, that it lengthens one's lifespan, that it eradicates anger, that it brings no harm to anyone, that it does not steal, that it does not lie, that it does not indulge in sexual misconduct, that it does not flatter or use harsh speech or become duplicitous, that it is not greedy or given to anger, that it is disconnected from all wrong views and wrong thoughts, that it always upholds the precepts, that it makes steady progress, that it aids meditation, that it increases prajna wisdom, and that it helps one fulfill the Six Paramitas.

4) Patience is the source or cause of bodhi wisdom. Patience under insult not only teaches us how to live among the beings in this world, it also teaches us how to become Buddhas ourselves. In the *Patience of Rahula Sutra* Buddha says, 'Due to the practice of patience, I have attained Buddhahood and am revered by all worlds. Freely, I travel throughout the three realms.'

The *Upasakashila Sutra* says:

> *Even if your body were being hacked to pieces, you still should not become angry; you should contemplate deeply the causes of this karma and practice compassion and kindness toward all beings. If you are unable to be patient in little things, how will you be able to do the great work of helping all sentient beings? Patience under insult is the main cause of awakening in the bodhi mind. Anuttara-samyak-sambodhi [complete enlightenment] is the result of being patient under insult. If you do not plant those seeds, then how can you expect to attain those results?*

How to Get Along With Others

Generosity, praise, good behavior
and fellowship: these four methods
will bring harmony to all the world.

— from the *Abidharma Samgiti Paryayapada*

None of us can live alone and none of us should want to. In this world it is impossible not to have many dealings with other people. If we are unskilled in the way we deal with others, our lives will be full of problems. If we are skilled, however, our lives will be full of joy. All of us need other people. We need to engage in healthy and productive relations with others. As soon as we recognize this basic fact of life, we will want to know how to be skillful in our relations with others. How should we behave so that we can always get along with other people? What should we do to promote both our own growth and the growth of others at the same time?

The *Abidharma Samgiti Paryayapada* says that the four methods described in the passage above provide an excellent foundation on which we can base all of our social behavior.

Generosity
Generosity is compassion in action. It is the bottom line. It is an excellent indicator of whether we are truly practicing Buddhists or not. You may be a great philosopher and very knowledgeable about Buddhist texts and Buddhist history, but if you are not being gener-

ous with your life then you are not really practicing Buddhism. If you have not yet learned how to give, you will not have the capacity to fully appreciate the depth of the Buddha's teachings.

Buddhist generosity can come in many different forms. We can be generous with our possessions, with our time, with our emotions, with our talents, with our wisdom, and with our joy. As Buddhists we should never be afraid to be generous. Once we begin to pay attention to this subject, we will find that every day we are presented with many opportunities to be generous in some way or another.

At its most basic level, generosity is active, positive energy directed toward another person in such a way that that person will feel joy or gain in wisdom. When we are generous we learn how to be unattached to our possessions or our beliefs, and we provide others with an example of human behavior that is not founded on greed.

The *Upasakashila Sutra* says that one who is frequently generous will gain five benefits: 1) he will never be far from the wise, 2) sentient beings will take delight in his presence, 3) he will not be afraid to be in large groups of people, 4) he will gain a good reputation, 5) he will increase his understanding of the bodhi mind.

Generosity is crucial to any vision of a harmonious world. One can become acquainted with the value of generosity through contemplation, but a full understanding of it only can come after one has learned to be generous with real people in this world.

Praise and encouragement

Praise lights up the mind and soothes the heart. Not only does praise provide its recipient with a moment of happiness, it also presents him with an enduring confirmation that his contribution to the world has been noticed and appreciated. All of us are social beings. We cannot live happily without the affection and respect of our fellow humans. When we give praise or encouragement to another, we strengthen the social bond between us and we empower that person to reach out beyond himself to yet others who surely also need the solace of friendship and the knowledge that others need them.

Praise is the opposite of insult. Encouragement is the opposite of the negative urge to undermine or harm others in the mistaken belief that their pain can ever be our joy. Just as we learn to be generous, so we must learn to praise and encourage others. Never hold back a kind word and never be stinting with warmth and encouragement. When you encourage others, you begin to mingle your energy with the great, transcendent energy that inspires and moves all the bodhisattvas and Buddhas in the universe.

The *Maharatnakuta* says that encouraging language is language that is born in a joyful mind and in a mind that is not defiled by selfish distinctions. This sutra says that encouraging language gives peace and comfort to all sentient beings and that it speeds the progress of all activities.

Shakyamuni Buddha was a master of praise and encouragement. Whenever he addressed others he always used phrases like "good men and good women" and whenever he preached the Dharma, he carefully chose his words so that his audience would feel encouraged to practice and hopeful about their futures. The very fact that he preached at all shows how concerned he was with the well-being of others. In a manner of speaking, the Dharma can be understood as the highest form of encouragement ever spoken by anyone in this world.

Good behavior

Good behavior is behavior that brings benefit both to oneself and to others. Good behavior depends on our being mindful of the actions of our bodies and minds and of our speech. When we use body, mind, and speech to help others, we are practicing good behavior.

The *Maharatnakuta* says that good behavior brings joy both to others and to oneself and that it is born deep within a mind that has nothing to regret. The sutra says that good behavior helps both oneself and others and that it is based on a profound understanding of the essential equality among all sentient beings. Good behavior is behavior that is focused primarily on the well-being of others. By always giving the best of ourselves to others, we raise the level of whatever social group we find ourselves in. Simultaneously, we succeed in uncovering the very deepest levels of ourselves. When we give to others, we awaken the greatest source of wisdom in the universe.

Fellowship

Fellowship can be defined as anything that brings us closer to others and helps us understand their joys and sorrows. By achieving close fellowship with the members of the society we live in, we improve our chances of influencing others for the better. We cannot lead others to the Dharma if we are ignorant of their needs, their fears and their joys.

The *Maha-ratnakuta* says that fellowship is that quality within us that leads us to use our wisdom and compassion to bring others to the Dharma. When we begin to understand the importance of sharing the Dharma with others and when we begin to act on this understanding, we can be sure that we are acting out of the deepest sources of fellowship. This is the very same source that inspired the Buddha to preach for forty-five years. When we sense this source even slightly, we can know that we are sensing the Buddha within. Insofar as we understand the need to lead others to the Dharma, we are the same as the Buddha.

> *The purpose of generosity is to strengthen*
> *the roots of the bodhi mind.*
> *The purpose of praise is to nurture*
> *the shoots of the bodhi mind.*
> *The purpose of good behavior is to cause*
> *Bodhi flowers to bloom.*
> *The purpose of fellowship is to*
> *ripen the fruits of bodhi wisdom.*
>
> — from the *Maharatnakuta*

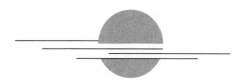

Friends

There are four kinds of friends,
this you must know.
One is like a flower, another like a scale.
One like a mountain, and one like the earth.

— from the *Fo Shuo Pei Sutra*

Everyone needs friends. As we recognize this need, it is important to recognize as well that not all friends are the same. Some friends help us grow while others hinder us and even seek to harm us. How are we to know the difference between good friends and harmful friends? The *Fo Shuo Pei Sutra* has some advice on this point. The sutra distinguishes four kinds of friends.

Friends who treat us as if we were flowers

In good times they place us on their heads.
If we wither, they throw us away.
If we are doing well, they treat us well.
If we become poor, they abandon us.

— from the *Fo Shuo Pei Sutra*

The sutra explains that people who are themselves like flowers will treat us like flowers, too. When we are blooming with wealth and good health and happiness, they will use us to decorate their lives. As soon as the bloom is gone, however, they will discard us like a wilted flower from a vase in their room. The metaphor of the flower is used to describe how transient and unreliable relations of that sort can be. Friends like that can appear very charming and attractive, but since they only want to associate with us for samsaric reasons, we should be wary and not allow ourselves to become overly attached to them.

All of us have had experiences with people like that. Having had those experiences, we should consider the harm and pain they caused us. Having considered that, we should determine that we ourselves will not be false in our own friendships.

Furthermore, when we read the sutra's description of friends who are like flowers, it is important that we not become judgmental. The sutra offers the metaphor of the flower only to protect us from harm, not to give us an excuse to do harm to others. All of us should be cautious about the people we choose to call our friends, but none of us should ever be judgmental or cruel. It is important to remember that some people who appear like flowers are that way only because they are socially awkward or because they are trying perhaps a little too hard to be our friend. And even if we do perceive that someone is only using us to decorate their own lives, we should not abandon them ourselves to prevent them from doing the same to us! It would be better if we took some time to share the Dharma with them and help them to raise their vision so that they might see the much more beautiful and truthful flower of the bodhi mind.

Friends who are like weighing scales

> *When we are heavy, they tip their heads.*
> *When we are light, they raise their heads.*
> *When we have possessions, they respect us.*
> *When we have nothing,*
> *they become haughty and proud.*

> — from the *Fo Shuo Pei Sutra*

Some friends are just like scales: if you are heavier than them, they will bow their heads to you. If you are lighter, they will raise themselves above you. Friends like this are constantly making judgments about us. They tend to understand life in terms of higher and lower. People of this sort generally base their judgments of others on their perceptions of social status and not on the deeper emotions which are the real sources of true friendship.

This very human tendency is quite common. The ancient caste system of India is based on a psychology that places some people above others. Racism springs from these same roots, as do most of the competitive and violent urges of human beings.

Sometimes friends who are like scales have opposite emotions to the ones described above; when we become heavy with success they become envious and angry, and when we become lightened by loss, they become friendly again. This type of friend is also looking at life through eyes focused mainly on samsaric status. This kind of person, however, seeks to lower others rather than raise himself.

If a friend begins to harbor feelings of envy toward us, what should we do? How should we deal with him? This is a difficult question to answer because there are many kinds of people and many kinds of envy. The difficulty of this problem is compounded by the fact that envy too often leads to anger or hatred. When friends who have secretly become angry with us conceal their anger under a mask of continuing friendship, this general problem has reached its most serious point.

The basic way to deal with angry or envious friends is practice patience and compassion and don't argue with them. Often this will cure the problem. If it does not, all we can do as Buddhists is continue to practice patience and compassion. It is not right to abandon our friends, but sometimes it is a good idea to put a little distance between yourself and your friend if you see that emotions between you are getting out of control. For the most part, it is intimacy between people that generates the strongest and most uncontrollable emotions. If we have tried the above methods but still we are harmed by a friend, then as Buddhists we still have only one recourse—to continue practicing patience and compassion.

All of us have need of the Dharma precisely because this world is not perfect. Friends fight, family members betray each other, and even love can turn to hate. The best way to prevent these kinds of negative conditions from developing between people is to often discuss the Dharma with each other. The Buddha's teachings contain everything we need to understand life; they are complete teachings and when friends often discuss the Dharma they protect themselves from being preyed upon by demonic emotions or controlled by unconscious levels of their personalities.

Friends who are like mountains

> Birds and beasts flock there
> as if to a golden mountain;
> their fur and feathers reflect its light.
> Greatness gives greatness to others
> and shares their joys and blessings.

— from the Fo Shuo Pei Sutra

Some friends are like great mountains. They are capable of supporting forests and animals on their slopes. They are tolerant of everything that passes over them and will allow anyone to live near them. They do not object to bad weather, and even after years of violent storms they remain largely unchanged. All of us should seek to be like this, and if we are fortunate enough to find friends like this, we should treat them with the utmost respect and consideration. Patience, tolerance, compassion and the ability to be a good friend are the traits of a Buddha and when they appear in people, they should be revered just as if they were aspects of the Buddha, for that is what they are.

Friends who are like the earth

> Great good fortune and great wealth
> cause all to offer their respects.
> If the wealthy one is generous and helpful,
> they all will be grateful as well.

— from the Fo Shuo Pei Sutra

Some friends are like the earth. They are patient and expansive. They can hold anything. They are a source of life and a foundation for all things to grow upon. In the verse above "great good fortune and great wealth" should be understood as describing someone who is talented and virtuous. When such a person is generous with his abilities, he will be like the earth in that many people will be able to learn from him and many people will be nourished by him. If such a person also happens to be wealthy, then he will be even more able to help others.

It is important that all of us strive to be like the mountains and earth in our friendships, and it is important that all of us fully appreciate these qualities in others whenever we discover them.

When you have found a true friend,
you have found the best thing in life
and life will no longer seem so evil.

— from the *Ekottarika Agama*

Friendship

If you handle the grass
a fish has been laid on,
your hand will smell like a fish;
and this is what it is like
to associate with evil friends.

— from the *Abhiniskramana Sutra*

The importance of friendship

Friends are important. There is little in life that is more important than the people we choose to call our friends. These are the people who help us grow and whom we are bound to help in return. Since friendship is based on a conscious choice, it is a relationship which is at once more difficult to establish than a family relation and frequently much more valuable.

Confucius said:

> *When we live with a good person, before long we stop*
> *noticing how he changes us for the better. It is as if we*
> *moved into a room full of orchids; before long we stop*
> *noticing their fragrance.*
>
> *When we live with a bad person, before long we stop*
> *noticing how he changes us for the worse. It is like enter-*
> *ing a fish market; before long we stop noticing how badly*
> *it smells.*

When we have good friends, we should always try to appreciate how much their company does for us, and we should never allow ourselves to forget what we have gained from them. At the same time, no one should be innocent about making friends. This world is full of many kinds of people, and many of those kinds are not good. If you have friends who are encouraging you to break the precepts of Buddhism, you would do well to look for new friends. We should do everything in our power to help others, but if their company is having a consistently bad effect on our behavior, we should realize that our relationship with them is not healthy and that it would probably be better to end it or at least diminish it greatly. Friends are very important to our growth and development, and for this reason we should exercise good care in our choosing of them.

The value of good friends
The *Sigalovada Sutra* says good friends have four basic characteristics:
   1) If they see us doing wrong, they will speak up.
   2) They are kind to us.
   3) They take joy in helping others.
   4) They do not abandon us in time of need.

These four points are quite important; they reveal very basic attitudes that are crucial not just for friendship, but also for making progress in Buddhism. Let's look at them a little more closely.

1) If they see us doing wrong, they will speak up.

A friend who does this will keep us from much harm. Remember, it is always good to have a second or third opinion concerning our behavior. A friend like this will probably also provide us with a good example in many situations: it is possible to learn a great deal about how to behave from our friends. A friend of this type is also certain to be a compassionate and thoughtful person; friends do not usually speak up unless they are thinking of our best interests. Good friends help us find our way out of delusion. They do not mislead us and they try to stop us when they see that we are being misled.

2) They are kind to us.

Kindness is the basis of friendship. Why would anyone be friends with someone who was not kind to them? Friends who are kind will take joy in our achievements and delight in our progress. At the same time, they will become anxious if they see that we are doing something wrong. They will not talk badly of us behind our back, and they will do whatever they are able to enhance our reputation. If they hear someone else speaking badly of us, they will defend us and put a stop to their disrespectful speech.

3) They take joy in helping others.

Friends like this will not hide away when we need their help and they will not lead us into making mistakes. They will never make us feel afraid, and when we speak with them we will always know that they are being honest. If our lives should improve in some way, they will not become jealous or seek to undermine us.

4) They do not abandon us in time of need.

Friends like this will never reveal secrets we have told them, or use what we have said to them to harm us behind our backs. They are constant in both time and space; we know that they will be our friends in the future and we know that they will behave as our friends even when we are not with them in the present.

Whenever we find a friend who resembles the above description, we should treasure him and reciprocate his kindness every chance we have. Friends of this type will bring us much good. They will help us grow more quickly than anything else in the world. Needless to say, all Buddhists should strive to be this type of friend to others.

The *Abhiniskramana Sutra* says, "If we dip our hands in *garu*-wood incense, or in musk or fragrant betony, in a moment our hands will pick up those odors; spending time with good people is just like this."

The danger of bad friends

The *Sigalovada Sutra* says there are four basic types of people who are bad friends: 1) friends who are greedy or who use fear to deceive, 2) friends who use flattery to get what they want, 3) friends who use a guise of respectfulness to flatter us, and 4) friends whose only purpose in friendship is to seek pleasure. Let's look more closely at these four types.

1) Friends who are greedy or who use fear to deceive.

This is the kind of person who always wants more from you. If you give him one thing, soon he will want another. When he helps you just a little, he expects you to repay him with a lot. This type of person often uses fear to manipulate people; he will draw you to him by trying to control you through feelings of guilt or fear. The basis of all his motivation is his own benefit, and little or nothing that he does with you or for you will spring from other causes.

2) Friends who use flattery to get what they want.

No matter what you do, this kind of person will praise you, but the moment you lose power or influence in society, he will abandon you. This kind of person is motivated by greed; when he sees that you have something he wants or that he can use you, he will draw close to you, flatter you, and ask for your help. He may seem like someone who is genuinely in need, but he is really only motivated by greed. The moment you need him, he will disappear.

3) Friends who use a guise of respectfulness to flatter you.

Friends like this will not warn you when they see that you are behaving badly, and they will not volunteer to help you when they see the opportunity to do so. When they see that they may have something to gain from you, they draw near. And when they see that there is nothing to gain, they move away.

4) Friends whose only purpose in friendship is to seek pleasure.

This type of person will spend time with you only when food or alcohol are being consumed, or when there is some other low activity to be indulged in like gambling, using drugs, sexual misconduct, or other frivolous stimulations of the senses.

Most people are mixtures of all of the good and bad tendencies we have described in this section. All of them are sentient beings and all of them are fully deserving of our compassion. Nevertheless, some people tend to be much worse than others. If you find yourself having frequent contact with a person who has many bad tendencies, you should protect yourself by keeping your distance if you feel that his tendencies are influencing you for the worse. The strongest single influence we have in life is the people we associate with often.

All of us should do our best to be good friends to those who associate with us. At the same time, we should look to be sure that we are spending our time with people whose influence on us is wholesome and elevating. Life is too short to be wasted wandering among the many low emotions this world is capable of offering us all the time.

If you spend your time with bad friends,
you will get nowhere in this life and
you will fall with the company you have kept
to the lower realms in your next life.

If you spend your time with good friends,
your karma will mingle with their good karma
and even if you appear to gain nothing in this life,
you will have created the causal conditions
for liberation from all suffering.

— from the *Abhiniskramana Sutra*

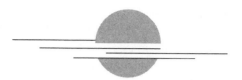

Gratitude

When someone benefits us even a little,
we should repay them with all our hearts.
Even if someone is angry with us,
we should always treat them well.

— from the *Upasakashila Sutra*

Gratitude is fundamental to Buddhism.

A natural outgrowth of heartfelt gratitude is the desire to repay others for the kind things they have done for us. Having the feeling of being indebted to others is a sign that we are aware of our essential interconnectedness with them. Human beings are social beings; once we have become sensitive to the depth of our social natures, we will inevitably feel the need to repay others for the many things they have given us and the many opportunities they have provided us with.

The Buddha himself is the best example we could ask for of someone who took joy in the joys of others and who gave all he could of himself for the good of others. The Buddha was never arrogant when he preached, and he never said things to frighten others away. Whenever we seek to give to others or to repay them out of a sense of gratitude, we should remember the Buddha's example.

Our attempts at kindness should not be received as burdens by the people for whom they are intended, nor should they cause us to feel arrogant or that thenceforth we may dismiss any bond we may have felt with the recipient. When we act on a desire to repay a kindness, we are not settling an account or cleaning a slate, we are deeply acknowledging the importance of someone else to us. By acknowledging this importance, we create conditions that will lead to a deepening of our relationship with that person.

Whenever we deepen our relations with others, we must not do so out of a sense of greed or attachment, and we must not expect anything in return. As our relationships with other sentient beings grow deeper and deeper, our awareness of the importance of gratitude can only increase. Eventually we will understand that there is no fundamental difference between gratitude, compassion, and wisdom; all of them are the same; each of them is a facet of the mind of the Tathagata.

To whom should we be grateful?

Buddhist sutras generally agree in saying that the four most important things we should be grateful for are: 1) the Triple Gem, 2) our parents, 3) our teachers and 4) our nations.

The *Saddharma Smriti Upasthana Sutra* mentions a slightly different list of four things that we should be grateful for. It says that we should be grateful to the Buddha, to the Sangha, to our fathers and to our mothers.

The *Contemplations on the Basis of Mind Sutra* says that we should be most grateful to our parents, to all sentient beings, to our nations, and to the Triple Gem.

The sutras list several things that we should be most grateful for to encourage us to realize how much we owe others. These short lists are not intended to encourage us to ignore everything else. As Buddhists, we should feel fundamentally grateful for everything that happens to us. We should be grateful that the sun shines, that the world turns, that our bodies are alive, and that we are aware and can read Dharma literature. We should be grateful to those who have helped us learn the Dharma and to the Sangha who maintain the Dharma. Above all we should be grateful to the Buddha who spent so many years generously giving sentient beings the teachings we have today.

How to be grateful
The *Ekottarika Agama* says:

> *When we repay a kindness done to us, we should be*
> *mindful of that kindness and the help it has brought us.*
> *Even small kindnesses should not be forgotten, much less*
> *large acts of kindness.*

True gratitude is a product of both instinct and thought. When we are in tune with our basic feelings, we will find that gratitude flows naturally from us. When we think deeply, we will understand that everything we are is dependent on others. Once our eyes have been opened, how can we possibly feel anything less than the most profound gratitude for everything that is around us?

The *Sutra on the Compassionate Upaya of the Buddha* says that we fulfill ourselves and repay our debt of gratitude toward the world by always being compassionate and doing our best to manifest the Four Immeasurable States of Mind of the Tathagata: boundless kindness, boundless compassion, boundless joy, and boundless equanimity.

The sutra continues its discussion of gratitude by mentioning four other ways of being that can help us always remain grateful toward the world. It says:

1) When we see an evil person, we should become thoughtful and consider that their evil is a burden most of all to themselves. With this understanding we should treat them with as much compassion as possible.

2) When we see someone who is suffering, we should not turn away from them. Instead we should bring them as much comfort as we are able.

3) When we are with our parents, our teachers, or others who are of good nature, we should feel joy and respect. We should seek to build on the compassion they have shown us by creating even more positive conditions in the world.

4) When we come upon someone who is angry with us, we should not return the feeling. Instead we should look for every way we can think of to diminish it.

All the great masters of the past understood the central importance of gratitude. Once our feelings of gratitude are fully developed, we will at last be in a position to absorb the deep fullness of the Buddha's teachings.

Master Yin Kuang (1862–1940) expressed this point very well. When Yin Kuang was twenty-one years old he entered a monastery where he was put to work as a water boy. Every day he had to fetch and boil water for the other monks in his monastery. When there was no fuel to heat the water, it was his duty to go into the hills to get more. His job was menial and difficult, and yet Yin Kuang felt nothing but joy for having the opportunity to do it at all. One day he said to the other monks, "You are all so good to me! You have allowed me to come here to be a monk and you have given me the opportunity to live and learn among you. It is so little, but I will do everything I can to repay you by being the best water boy I can be."

Master Yin Kuang's attitude was so deep and so true to his inner nature, it was an expression of the Buddha within. How many of us would have grumbled and been discontented if we had been given his job? Imagine that there had been two monks assigned to fetch and boil water at the monastery. And imagine that one of them complained and shirked his duties while the other was Yin Kuang. Which of them do you think would have learned the fastest?

To be like Master Yin Kuang, all we must do is follow his example in our own lives, no matter what our conditions are.

How to repay someone who is discontented

Simply having a well-developed sense of gratitude does not mean that we will never be around people who are negative, angry, impatient or discontented. The bodhisattva lives in this world with all its many different kinds of people. As Buddhists we must learn to deal with each and every one of them.

Once we have a sense of gratitude, a willingness to be forgiving of others should quickly follow. Gratitude and forgiveness are great aids to overcoming the ups and downs of human moods and human relationships. When we have learned these virtues, it will be possible for us to be tolerant and compassionate toward others in all circumstances.

When someone is negative, we should be positive. When someone is angry, we should try to be kind. When someone is impatient, we should be patient. And when someone is discontented, we should help them feel contented. Don't let yourself get hooked on other people's negative emotions. If their emotions are negative in general, try to be positive. If their negative emotions are specifically directed at you, try to always answer them with forgiveness, kindness, and compassion. The moment we allow ourselves to become engaged in any kind of negativity, our worlds immediately become darker.

The *Avadanas* says, "Do not repay anger with anger. One day there must be a stop." The *Vimalakirti Nirdesha Sutra* says that we should not allow ourselves to dwell on the transgressions of our friends.

The Buddha said:

> *Good monks, all sentient beings*
> *eventually will enter Nirvana.*
> *It is only due to their unmet needs that*
> *their minds are disordered and thus they do not attain it.*
> *Good monks, all sentient beings*
> *delight in learning and changing for the better,*
> *but since their minds are harassed by their cares,*
> *they do not attain concentration*
> *and they do not attain Nirvana now.*

> — from the *Mahaparinirvana Sutra*

Beyond Differentiation

Do not insult others and do not judge them;
simply observe yourself in the light of truth.

— from the *Ekottarika Agama*

Buddhism is based on human nature. There is no question concerning human behavior that cannot be answered by the Dharma. Everything is covered. Incidentally, this is one of the reasons why it is good for Buddhists to ask questions; you might not get them answered immediately, but eventually you will.

The *Ekottarika Agama* makes four basic points about the universal human tendency to judge other people or to differentiate among them. These points will be discussed in detail in the next four sections.

Do not insult others

"Mount T'ai does not reject a single clod of earth and so it is tall. The ocean accepts all streams which flow into it and so it is vast."

This saying beautifully portrays the important truth that none of us should reject others, or judge them, or demean them, or reduce them in any way. It is easy to understand this truth, but difficult to practice what it teaches. To understand ourselves, we must look closely at what nearly all of us actually do quite often. We look at someone and decide we don't like them, or we hear them say something we don't like and decide they are not wise enough to be in our company. Then we avoid them. This is the first step in what the sutra has called 'insulting others.' In polite society, insults are rarely verbalized. However, whenever we give someone the cold shoulder, are we not insulting them without words? Now look more deeply at why we avoid people. There are three basic reasons: the first is that we feel they have insulted or will insult us; the second is that they threaten us because we feel that they may be better than us in some way; and the third is that we feel we are better than them. These are dangerous attitudes or tendencies, and they are extremely deleterious to the practice of Buddhism. Any one of these attitudes involves a mistaken judgment of others, plus a mistaken judgment of ourselves! Whenever we feel jealousy, anger, or the need to avoid or insult someone, it is almost always a result of our having misjudged both ourselves and the other person.

Karma and the conditions of the world we live in bring us into contact with other people. Brace yourself if you must, but face your own tendencies to judge and insult others. Never let your own fear or hostility control your behavior. Whatever lesson is before you will stay before you until you have learned it; you will not grow as a Buddhist through insult and rejection of others. This is certain.

> *The minds of sentient beings*
> *have inner and outer parts.*
> *Whatever they grasp grasps them*
> *and forces them to see what they see.*

> — from the *Vijnaptimatratasiddhi Shastra*

Do not judge others

If we never judged others, we would never feel the need to insult them or avoid them. Buddhism begins and ends in the mind. Your mind is your own. If you find insults, anger, and hostility circulating inside it, do you really think you can blame that on the world? Is it really someone else's fault that you cannot control your own jealousy or moodiness? No one can look into your own mind except you. No one can make you progress in your practice of Buddhism except you. If you want to progress, do as the sutra says without making exceptions. I promise that you will progress rapidly in this way.

Now, why do we discriminate among people at all? The basic reason is we carry with us the illusion of having a separate self. This illusion maintains itself by making judgments. When illusions which are precious to us are threatened, we react with jealousy or anger or insult. The heart of the matter is that we are afraid. Our illusions are afraid. Once we understand this, it becomes possible to understand how to appreciate and use anger and jealousy for our own benefit. We cannot repress these emotions, and it would be foolish to pretend that they were not there. Buddhism is based on human nature. If these emotions are part of what it is to be human, we should be able to use them to advance in our practice.

If we understand that anger and jealousy are part of the illusion of having a separate self, then we will be ready to understand that each time these emotions occur they are signs which point directly at our own illusions. Anger is like pointing your finger at yourself in the mirror. Jealousy shows very precisely how much investment we have made in our own self-created egos. How could you feel jealous of anyone if you truly realized that all sentient beings and all Buddhas are the same? When friends do well, we should be pleased that they have been able to grow. Just as jealousy is a sign of our delusive limitations, our friends' growth is a sign that in some small way our company has encouraged them or helped them. Rather than be jealous of our friends, it is better to let them return the favor to us. When friends overcome jealousy among themselves and help each other to grow, enormous and very powerful energies are released.

> *Attention is dependent on awareness.*
> *If the roots of awareness are defiled,*
> *attention will never be free.*
>
> *If goodness is not obstructed*
> *and the mind is not clinging,*
> *and if the self is beyond grasping*
> *then there will be no defilements anywhere.*

> — from the *Vijnaptimatratasiddhi Shastra*

Observe yourself
The Buddha said, "After meditation and introspection, do not talk in terms that judge others." Introspection must be founded in honesty. If it is not, it will become nothing but another part of the illusion of having a separate self. Dishonest introspection leads to anger and deluded self-justification. If we are deluded, how do we know we are deluded? We can know we are deluded if we have the symptoms of delusion: anger, jealousy, and a strong tendency to judge others.

"After meditation and introspection, do not talk in terms that judge others." Preserve your peace. Abide in a state of mind devoid of petty distinctions and self-serving versions of the "truth." With practice, this will become your basic state of mind.

> *Shui Yen asked, 'And what of the great sword that*
> *has not been sharpened?' Master Hsing Sze replied, 'It*
> *cannot be used.' Shui Yen then asked, 'And what of the*
> *great sword that has been sharpened?' Master Hsing Sze*
> *replied, 'It cannot be touched.'*

> —from the Zen canon

In the light of truth
The *Lankavatara Sutra* says, "If the cause is not right, the result will be bad." The Dharma contains the truth and it is the truth. The Dharma is an endless companion and a perfect standard to help us understand everything that happens to us. All of us must constantly check and recheck ourselves in the light of the truths contained in the Dharma. If we are honest with ourselves, we will grow very quickly in our practice of Buddhism.

> *The compassion of the Tathagata*
> *is the summation of the Dharma.*
> *This compassion has the power*
> *to save all sentient beings because*
> *it is the supreme truth that leads*
> *to liberation in Nirvana.*

> — from the *Mahaparinirvana Sutra*

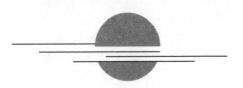

Helping

Do not think only of your own joy,
but vow to save all beings from suffering.
This is sharing in its highest form and
purity beyond all poisons of this world.

— from the *Avatamsaka Sutra*

Helping others and helping yourself

There are basically four ways we can look at the art of helping:

1) Helping others, but not helping yourself.
2) Helping yourself, but not helping others.
3) Helping neither yourself nor others.
4) Helping both yourself and others.

The first possibility mentioned above is fundamentally a contradiction in terms. The bodhisattva understands that self and others are one being. If you help others, you must be helping yourself. In this world, however, it sometimes does appear as if someone is helping others while bringing no help to himself. As long as this sort of compassion is not a mask for self-abuse, it is a beautiful and rare occurrence. It is always the behavior of one who is inspired by the highest truths of life. The mental and moral growth of anyone who performs any deed in this consciousness will be very great and it will be inevitable.

Helping the self without helping others also contains a basic contradiction since it is not ultimately possible to help the self without helping others. In this *saha* world, however, it often appears to be possible to get more than we give and it often appears to be desirable to do so. This is the reasoning of delusion. As long as you feel that this kind of reasoning has any hold on you, you can be sure that your awareness still has room to grow. There is nothing to be gained in delusion and delusive reasoning will not lead you to the truth.

Shakyamuni Buddha understood this truth better than anyone and that is why he gave forty-five years of his life to preaching the Dharma. He taught the bodhisattva way and he lived it. He taught all of us who follow him the compassionate way to liberation from suffering. This way is based on helping both the self and others at the same time. When one understands the truth of compassion and the wisdom of bringing aid to others, the bodhisattva way opens before one as the only natural course in the world. How could there be another way? How could it be right to help yourself without helping others?

The bodhisattva's commitment to others is both emotional and wise. When both wisdom and emotion are directed toward the same goal, nothing can prevent its attainment. There is nothing stronger in the world. Fan Chung-yen of the Sung dynasty (960–1278) said, "Think firstly of those who suffer in this world and have compassion for them. Think secondly of the joys of this world and share them."

Amitabha Buddha's vow to help both himself and others at the same time was so great it was a sufficient cause for the creation of his Pure Land. Kshitigarbha Bodhisattva vowed, "Until hell is empty, I will not become a Buddha." The compassion and determination which produced this vow is truly amazing. This is the highest level of strength a bodhisattva is capable of. Strength based on dedication to others is so wonderful the mere thought of it must move the heart. All of us should frequently contemplate the depths of compassion that produce vows of this nature. Few of us can expect to reach these depths ourselves, but all of us can benefit from contemplating the strength and generosity of those who have.

Sharing in its highest form
Sharing is a kind of generosity or compassion. In its highest form, sharing entails sharing ourselves. When we share the best of our-

selves—our best wisdom, our best thoughts, our best feelings—we make a gift of ourselves to the world. The giving of this kind of gift must be done with complete humility. We must clear our minds of illusions about ourselves or preconceptions about other people. To share the best of ourselves means simply to give our best at all times.

Sharing of this kind is one of the most wonderful methods of all for practicing Buddhism. It can be likened to using the flame of a candle in our own hand to light the wick of a candle held in another's. Our action does not diminish at all the light of our own candle; it only increases the amount of light available for everyone.

We could also compare sharing to planting a seed. In the moment it may appear that a few seeds have been lost, but soon it will become apparent that a whole harvest has been gained. When we share, we lose nothing. We only gain. Whenever we share, we transmit positive energy to others in such a way that all beings everywhere are improved by the act.

The *Commentary on the Avatamsaka Sutra* describes ten basic kinds of sharing:

1) Taking from ourselves and giving to others. In this form of sharing we especially give our merits to others.

2) Taking the small and giving to the many. In this we use our small abilities and small accumulation of merit to do our best to benefit sentient beings everywhere.

3) Taking from the selfish path and giving to the great path. In this we use our small realizations gleaned from lesser paths and contribute them to the great path of Mahayana Buddhism.

4) Taking small causes and turning them into great results. In this we recognize that all phenomena spring from causes. Rather than placing our attention on the results of past karma manifesting now, we place our attention on the causes we are creating now; these causes ultimately will result in great goodness for all sentient beings if we are properly mindful of them now.

5) Taking the imperfect and making it perfect. The bodhisattva is able to adapt to the ways of ordinary people in order to lead them toward the highest truths.

6) Taking all the troubles and details of this world and turning them into the means of enlightenment. In humanistic Buddhism especially, we do not ignore the realities of this world and we do not turn our backs on others. On the contrary, we use the trials of this life to hone our practice and make us fit to be a benefit to all beings everywhere.

7) Taking the events of this life and turning them into the truths of an enlightened mind. We must learn to see everything that happens in this world as a manifestation of a higher truth that is neither born nor dies.

8) Taking differences and seeing in them the one. We must learn to see the underlying unity of all sentient beings and of all phenomena. This is the vision of the unobstructed Dharma that flows everywhere.

9) Taking the mundane and seeing in it the transcendental. All goodness practiced in this world becomes a means for transcending this world. Knowledge of transcendental truths is an important basis for teaching and helping others.

10) Taking the ultimate truths of the Dharma and applying them to the events and phenomena of this world. This is a perfect summation of the task of the bodhisattva. A bodhisattva is a conduit for transcendental truths and a standard in this world of the perfection of the Dharma.

How to practice sharing

True sharing is selfless. It is a flow of energy between the "self" and the "world." Since ultimately both "self" and "world" are empty, sharing itself can be said to be nothing more than higher awareness. Like compassion it is an aspect of the enlightened mind.

"All glory to Buddha, all benefit to others, all strength to the monastery, all merit to benefactors." When one is truly inspired to share, one keeps nothing for oneself since the self is entirely lost in the act of sharing. All of us should spend some time every day contemplating how much of our lives already are based on sharing with others. Our food, clothing, motor vehicles, jobs, language, education, and even our deep psychology are entirely dependent on sharing; without the contributions of other people we would be bereft of all of them. When we recognize this sharing from a Buddhist point of view, we begin to feel as if we are floating among the commingling energies of other people and other things. This is a true picture of reality. We are, all of us are, those other beings and things: in reality, there is no separation between us.

The *Lotus Sutra* contains the following lines, which can be chanted whenever one feels that something good may have been accomplished:

> *I hope that whatever*
> *merit has accrued from this deed*
> *will spread to all beings in the universe.*
> *And I hope that all sentient beings,*
> *including myself,*
> *will all achieve Buddhahood.*

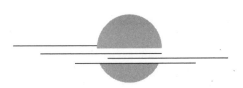

The Way to Help Others

Compassion is the father,
the bodhi mind the mother.
Good methods are like friends
because they save all sentient beings.

—from the *Great Collection of True Dharmas Sutra*

Compassion is the father

Compassion removes suffering and creates joy. The sutra says, "The power of the Dharma is beyond expression. Nothing can obstruct compassion."

Compassion is the root source of all good. Compassion is the heart of Buddhism. Compassion is an emotion. It is a state of mind. It is the bodhi mind. It is the Buddha nature and it is the ultimate reality. Compassion is truth in its purest form.

The sutras repeat this many times in many different places. They say, "Compassion is first," or "Compassion is the source," or "The bodhisattva is born of compassion and not from anything else."

In human life, all of us have been created from the seed of our fathers. Without that seed we would not be here. In the same way, without the seed of compassion, growth into the fullness of the Buddha nature is not possible and thus the *Ta Chihui Cheng Fa Sutra* says, "Compassion is the father."

The *Avatamsaka Sutra* says that there are ten conditions that lead ·
to the birth and growth of compassion: 1) Recognizing that we depend

on and are part of all sentient beings; 2) Recognizing that sentient beings are disturbed at their very cores; 3) Recognizing that sentient beings lack goodness; 4) Recognizing that sentient beings are as if asleep in a long night; 5) Recognizing that sentient beings do many kinds of bad things; 6) Recognizing that sentient beings are ruled by their desires and passions; 7) Recognizing that sentient beings are sunk deep in the sea of birth and death; 8) Recognizing that sentient beings suffer greatly; 9) Recognizing that sentient beings do not want to do good; 10) Recognizing that sentient beings are far from the Dharma.

It is well worth spending some time thinking about these ten conditions. Sentient beings are deluded, angry and very often unfriendly. If we are going to help them, it is important not to have too many illusions about them before we begin.

The bodhi mind is the mother

The bodhi mind is that part of us which seeks to grow toward the Buddha nature as it simultaneously tries to help others. If we want to grow morally only so that we can reap rewards for ourselves, then we will go to heaven where we will spend a long time amidst pleasant surroundings. Eventually, however, we will fall back into one of the lower realms. If we want to grow morally only to release ourselves from the cycle of birth and death, then we will miss the highest turn in the road. Our consciousness will remain on a lower plane for a very long time. The *Avatamsaka Sutra* says, "One who loses sight of the bodhi mind and yet tries to cultivate goodness will fall prey to demonic forces."

The bodhi mind is the middle path that seeks the benefit of the self and others at the same time. Just as a mother must feed and care for herself in order to care for her child, so the bodhi mind seeks its own growth even as it expends great energy to help others.

The bodhi mind is like a compassionate mother
because she bears and raises all bodhisattvas.

— from the *Avatamsaka Sutra*

Good methods are like good friends
Good friends help each other and do not let each other down. Any good method that leads sentient beings closer to the truth can be compared to a good friend since its basic purpose is to help.

The wise methods of Buddhism are capable of lifting all sentient beings out of the ocean of suffering. Buddha taught the Four Noble Truths for this purpose. He also taught the Three Dharma Seals for this same purpose. These, plus the Noble Eightfold Path, are absolutely essential to the practice and understanding of Buddhism. Once one is well grounded in these, one can begin to uphold the Five Precepts, progress in the Four Immeasurable States of Mind and realize truth via the Ten Wholesome Deeds.

Beyond these wise methods, Buddhism contains many other trail markers that lead us toward a realistic appreciation of conscious reality. These include the Thirty-Seven Conditions Leading to Buddhahood and the Fifty-Two Stages of the Bodhi Way among many others. Buddha showed us many ways to understand life. We may understand these ways one at a time or we may take them together. The important thing to remember is that compassion is always the source of everything. As the Buddha said:

> *The bodhisattva is great beyond words.*
> *Why do I say that? Because the bodhisattva*
> *knows very deeply that birth and death*
> *result from and cause all manner of*
> *transgression. The bodhisattva contemplates*
> *Nirvana and the greatness of it. He compares*
> *Nirvana to the cycle of birth and death*
> *in which sentient beings are trapped*
> *and in which they suffer immensely*
> *and he does not turn away from them.*
> *This is why I say the bodhisattva*
> *is great beyond all words.*

— from the *Mahaparinirvana Sutra*

Five Kinds of Inhumanity

When he ought to smile, he does not smile.
When he ought to feel joy, he feels none.
When he ought to be compassionate, he is not.
When he discovers his own mistakes,
he does not correct them.
When he hears of good things, he does not feel glad.

— from the *Ekottarika Agama*

Don't be like that! We should all learn to express our emotions simply, openly, and directly. Of course, no one should be ostentatious with his feelings, but expressing things you do not feel or not expressing things you do feel are most certainly forms of lying. Help one another and let life flow joyfully in you and through you. Those who learn to be in touch with the ordinary feelings of life will always be happiest.

Making friends

Our friends are the few people that we know in this immense universe. Treasure the ones you have and always be open to making new ones. In Buddhism, the concept of friendship is very deep and very important because it also involves the concept of karma. It is no accident that the people around you are who they are; some of them certainly are friends from former lives, all of them certainly will be friends in future lives. Each one of them has something to teach you.

Their relationship to you is very important, just as your relationship to them is very important. Therefore, do not play games with your friends; do not conceal your feelings and do not use emotion to manipulate others or to dominate any situation.

Smile when you ought to smile, be happy when you should be happy and give love wherever you feel it. Emotions are not things which should be calculated, hoarded or spent for some improper purpose.

When our emotional language is kept simple and straightforward, we will be able to make good friends and we will be able to make much faster progress in our practice of Buddhism. Blocked or constricted emotions are a major hindrance to growth in any endeavor, and especially in Buddhism.

> One day a monk who was lecturing on the Avatamsaka Sutra in Ch'ang-an asked Master Chih Wei, 'What does it mean in the sutras when it says that a sentient being's true nature is born only of conditions?'
>
> Master Chih Wei was silent and did not answer.
>
> Then his attendant stood up and said, "Virtuous monk, the moment you ask that question, or any question, in that moment your true nature is born of conditions."
>
> At this, the monk who had asked the question became enlightened.
>
> — from the Zen canon

Compassion

Compassion is so important in the practice of Buddhism that it can be thought of in many different ways. We can conceive of compassion as an ideal or we can personalize it in the form of a bodhisattva. We can use it as the standard of our practice of Buddhism or we can consider compassion to be an emotion. At the emotional level, compassion can become very powerful and indiscriminate. The more you understand the human condition, the less blockage there will be for a constant outflowing of compassion toward all sentient beings everywhere. To know yourself is to know others. Once you understand the complexity and beauty of human needs, you will naturally begin to sympathize with all forms of life no matter where they are.

Compassion is a teacher. Honestly felt and honestly expressed, it will never lead you astray. Let it teach you. This is how to practice Buddhism. When we speak of humanistic Buddhism, essentially we mean nothing more than this. Humanistic Buddhism is Buddhism that is practiced with and among other people. The standard of this practice, its method and its goal, is nothing more than compassion.

If you allow your compassion and your natural human emotions to flow naturally in the world around you, you will find it easy to get along with others and soon you will find that you are in a position to bring great help to them. The Buddha pointed out the five kinds of inhumane behavior because he wanted to show us through negative examples how we should behave in this world.

Correcting our own mistakes

Some people learn that they have been mistaken and they only know how to get mad! How foolish! We should be joyful when we learn of our own mistakes for now we can change for the better. Life is growth. Human life is a chance to grow to the highest levels of consciousness. How can anyone be angry at any chance to learn? Seize each chance to grow and never cling to an erroneous outlook or method just because you have become accustomed to it.

Start each day with the full knowledge that you are not perfect and then receive whatever correction the day has to offer you. Take it and change. Not only will you be a much happier person, but so will all of your friends.

It is a very simple and obvious point, but one that is well worth remembering—you cannot progress in Buddhism if you are unwilling to change.

> *All people have made many mistakes.*
> *If one is not repentant,*
> *one dulls one's own mind*
> *and calls retribution on oneself.*

> — from the *Sutra of Forty-Two Sections*

Hearing of good things

Emotions can be troublesome if we believe they must be concealed and controlled, or they can be our greatest ally if we understand that they can show us things about ourselves that we will never find inside our heads. One of the greatest blocks to a healthy outflow of emotion is envy or jealousy. When we feel envy instead of pleasure at someone else's accomplishments, we harm ourselves more than anyone. Envy blocks the natural heightening of awareness that arises when people close to us feel good or when they accomplish something worthwhile.

If we catch ourselves "hearing of good things and not feeling glad," we can be pretty sure that we are allowing envy or anger to control us. Under the control of anger, we are not able to grow quickly and may bring great harm to ourselves. If we are stuck in a negative emotional response, what should we do? The best thing is to fully and deeply reflect on your emotions as soon as you have time. Detailed abstract analysis is not what is called for here. Rather, you should simply allow yourself to feel all of your emotions completely and without censorship. My guess is you will discover much deeper and richer layers in yourself than you had thought were there. Oftentimes envy is nothing more than a twisted image of the joy you really do feel for others.

In the *Maha-parinirvana Sutra*, the Buddha said, "All sentient beings have their own natures and they all are different. Each one is unique." The way to progress in Buddhism is to understand this. Plumb your own nature. Then grant that others are different from you; different, but every bit as complex.

> *The bodhi mind is like a seed*
> *for it gives birth to the Dharma.*
> *The bodhi mind is like a good field*
> *for it nurtures all good phenomena.*
> *The bodhi mind is like a great land*
> *for it can hold everything at all times.*
> *The bodhi mind is like pure water*
> *for it can cleanse all troubles and pain.*
>
> — from the *Avatamsaka Sutra*

True Stature

True stature is not created by form or ornament;
words spoken out of jealousy and greed oppose it.
Only when evil has been stopped at its roots,
and when there is wisdom without anger
is there true stature.

—from the *Dharmapadavadana Sutra*

The false stature of this world

Everyone wants to be well regarded by others. However, in seeking true stature, people too often waste their time in the vain pursuit of its many imitations in this *saha* world; they seek after forms of social status, not true stature of the heart. They buy expensive clothes, expensive homes, and expensive cars in an effort to prove to others that they are worthy of respect. The truth, of course, is that no amount of money can buy true stature. True stature is an inner achievement; when a person has true stature it emanates from him without any effort on his part.

The false stature of false manners

All of us know that there are many people in the world who appear to be kind and friendly, but who have hearts that are full of jealousy and rage. They smile and say fine things to your face, but all the while they are only planning to bring you harm. People of this type have learned to act in such a way that they appear to be good when in fact they are not. They have confused the appearance of goodness with its essence. Their attempts to use this appearance for evil ends can never succeed in the long run.

True stature arises from within

The ancients said, "Integrity is within, form is without." If we want to achieve true stature, we must first look within. Within ourselves we will find the causes for all that happens to us. Every time we correct our mistaken thoughts, we raise ourselves to a higher stature. Every time we admit our own transgressions, we improve our chances to grow toward well-being. Every time we replace greed with non-attachment, we free ourselves of one more samsaric encumbrance.

> Once we fully overcome attachment
> and all of its ways of thought,
> then we will clearly understand that
> all goodness and all defilement
> arise dependent on inner conditions.

> — from the Treatise on the Awakening of Faith in the Mahayana

The highest stature

> The Bodhi mind is like a beautiful flower
> and all sentient beings love to gaze upon it.

> — from the Avatamsaka Sutra

The bodhi mind has no need of samsaric ostentation because it is completely beautiful in and of itself. The highest stature anyone can achieve is complete enlightenment within the fullness of the bodhi mind. This is the goal of all Buddhism.

The bodhi mind is the Buddha nature. The bodhi mind transcends all form, all attachment, all temptation to believe in a false self. A mere glimpse of the bodhi mind is sufficient to destroy the very roots of vanity. True stature is found only in this truth.

The bodhi mind is like a magnificent sun
for it shines on all things in the world.
The bodhi mind is like a full moon
for all dharmas find completion in it.

— from the *Avatamsaka Sutra*

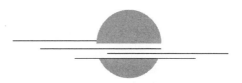

True Wisdom

He takes no delight in being shown respect.
If he is slighted, he shows no anger.
His wisdom is like an ocean.
These are the hallmarks of the truly wise.

— from the *Sutra on the Principles of the Six Paramitas*

Taking no delight in being shown respect
Buddhists often say that there are three basic worldly attachments
that each one of us must overcome to be truly successful in our
practice. The first is the attachment to fame, the second is the
attachment to wealth, and the third is the attachment to respect. For
most people, the labor of overcoming their attachments to fame and
wealth is much easier than the labor of overcoming their attachment
to respect.

Our desire to be respected is a basic animal instinct. In recognizing this, we must also recognize that this desire lies very deep within us and that it is fundamentally animalistic.

The *Mahaprajnaparamita Shastra* describes the Buddha as follows:

> *No matter how much evil and calumny were heaped*
> *upon him, the Buddha remained without evil thoughts*
> *himself. No matter how much praise and respect he was*
> *given, the Buddha remained unmoved by pleasure or*

delight. He looked on everything with a magnificent
compassion and saw friendship and enmity as one.

The desire to be respected is born, in part, from healthy social urges that are the motivating forces behind our learning, our friendships, our professions, and even our desire to study the Dharma. Buddhism is a religion that is learned progressively and many of the truths it elucidates can only be understood by comprehending that truth itself comes in levels. There is no one blanket rule that covers everything. Life is too complex for that. Our need to be respected should be understood as a need that has several different levels.

If we had no need for respect, we might not ever learn to speak, and certainly would never learn basic manners. This is the first level of our desire to be respected, and it produces mostly good results. The second level of our need to be respected begins to show when we start competing with others; first we want to be as good as them, but soon we want to be better. This level is a mixture of good and bad. The desire to compete can have good effects if it is well controlled and disastrous effects if it is not.

The third level of respect is the beginning of wisdom. At this level we begin to understand what respect is and where our desires for it have come from. Having seen this we see as well that these desires are fundamentally empty. We progress at this level first by contemplating the past and then by contemplating the timeless joy of the Buddha within.

In contemplating the past we learn by considering times in our own lives when we have craved respect or done something evil to obtain it. Would we do the same thing now? If not, then we have gained a place from which to observe our present desire for respect. If we can see the emptiness of the past, we should be able to see the emptiness of the present as well. Once we are able to see the emptiness of our present desire for respect, then nothing can obstruct our power to contemplate the perfection of the Buddha within. One glimpse of this perfection will clear away all remaining defilements.

Having no anger if you are insulted
The *Maha-prajna-paramita Sastra* says:

> Ordinary people become angry if they are intruded upon
> and they become happy if they are given some benefit. If
> they are in a frightening place, they become scared. If
> you want to be a bodhisattva, you must not be like that.
> Even though you have not broken all of the fetters which
> hold you to this world, still you must learn to control
> yourself by practicing patience under insult, not becom-
> ing angry when harmed or bothered, not becoming
> delighted when shown respect, and not becoming fright-
> ened by the sufferings and trials of this world.

As we progress in Buddhism, the ideal behavior of the bodhisattva
becomes clearer in our minds. We may still feel the strains and hardships of this world, but with our knowledge of the ideal, we learn to
create some distance between those strains and ourselves. We learn
to compare ourselves to something higher than what we have always
been and we learn to change for the better. Even one step on this
path will bring immense rewards, and anyone who takes two or three
steps will never turn back again.

When the means lead to higher awareness, we learn that the
means and the goal are one. The *Diamond Sutra* says:

> Good men and good women who persevere in chanting
> and reading this sutra: realize that if you can bear insults
> in this life without becoming angry or upset, then any
> bad karma you may have remaining from past incarna-
> tions will be eradicated and you will soon attain
> anuttara samyak sambodhi [the highest enlightenment].

No one in this world can possibly avoid being insulted. The conditions of our time and place are often turbulent, violent, and humil-
iating. Rather than permit these basic conditions to weaken our
resolve to improve ourselves, we should use them as opportunities to
strengthen our practice of Buddhism. The Buddha never asked us to

flee this world; he taught us to understand it and deal with it. If you are insulted, understand the conditions which produced the insult and deal with them compassionately. This is the way to grow.

Wisdom as vast as the sea

The *Mahaparinirvana Sutra* says:

> *When you think everything is someone else's fault, you*
> *will suffer a lot. When you realize that everything springs*
> *only from yourself, you will learn both peace and joy.*
> *Pride leads to violence and evil. The truly good gaze*
> *upon everything with love and understanding.*

It takes great wisdom to understand that the entire world springs from the mind.

The *Saddharma Smriti Upasthana Sutra* says, "Wisdom is the sweetest dew, the most peaceful refuge, the best friend and the greatest treasure." Wisdom allows us to continue our learning through all manner of hardship. It takes faith to become a Buddhist, but it takes wisdom to become a Buddha.

The *Avatamsaka Sutra* says, "Take refuge in the Dharma, vow to save all sentient beings, study the sutras deeply and you will attain wisdom as vast as the ocean."

Wisdom is achieved through study of the Dharma and contemplation on the inherent purity of the Buddha who lies within you.

> *All monks and all others*
> *progress through studying the Dharma.*
> *Whether sitting or walking,*
> *they read and chant this sutra.*
> *Even if they are in a forest*
> *seated under a tree*
> *and concentrating in deep meditation,*
> *those who uphold this sutra will*
> *sense a fragrance in the air*
> *and know that the Tathagata is near.*

> — from the *Lotus Sutra*

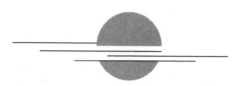

Blessings and Joys

To have no illness is the greatest blessing.
To be satisfied with what you have
is the greatest good fortune.
Good friends are the best of all relatives.
Nirvana is the supreme peace.

— from the *Magnificent Life of the Prince Sutra*

All of us want to live joyfully. The above quote teaches us everything we need to know about how to do this. People it seems, though, want to make life more complicated than it is. They look for complex ways to experience joy, and in doing so gradually twist their emotional responses so much that their innate abilities to love life are slowly lost. They abandon joy to the future by chasing money and status now, or bury joy in the present under an excess of sensuality and a deficiency of clear thought. Gradually, they become slaves to their own illusions. You can see it happening: their bodies start to seem weighted down and their expressions become worried and inattentive. If you speak to them they will have reasons for their ways, but their logic will be tangled and torn by the grip of samsara. True joy is found in purity of mind and study of the Dharma. Nothing else will bring it about.

Good health is the greatest blessing
All of us have had the experience of truly appreciating our health only after it was gone. Good health, like life itself, is a transient phenom-

enon. It is a positive condition that should be used to the fullest extent of our ability. It will not last forever. While we are in the midst of health, it is good to remember that our health is precious and that we do not have an unlimited amount of time to enjoy it. A healthy body provides the means to study, meditate, and learn the Dharma. It is only in this human realm that we can grow to our fullest potential.

The *Buddha's Medicine Sutra* says that there are ten basic reasons why people become ill: 1) sitting for long periods without eating, 2) overeating, 3) anxiety, 4) extreme fatigue, 5) excessive sensuality, 6) anger, 7) not excreting when needed, 8) not urinating when needed, 9) suppressing eructations, 10) not relieving the flatus.

The *Contemplations on the Basis of Mind Sutra* says, "Treat your body like a newborn baby. Comfort and care for it with the compassion of a mother. Watch over it carefully. If you do not care for your mind and body well and treat their illnesses, then you will not gain much enlightenment."

The health of our bodies affects our ability to practice and learn the Dharma. At the same time, the health of our minds affects the condition of our bodies. If we allow ourselves to be angry and impatient, our sleep will be disturbed and our nerves will suffer from overexertion. The ultimate source of good health, as with everything else, is the mind. If our minds are engaged in learning and practicing Buddhism, our bodies will tend to be healthy. If our minds are allowed to wander among violent and degrading emotions, then our bodies will tend to become unhealthy. Mental and physical health are interconnected.

Be satisfied with what you have

When a human being allows his desires to grow beyond all reasonable bounds, he becomes like a snake trying to swallow an elephant. No one needs that much. Unreasonable desires are born of illusion and greed. Being satisfied with whatever we have is an important step toward wisdom.

Greed narrows our vision as it obscures the wealth of wisdom contained in our inherent Buddha nature. Greed is always based on false premises. It always makes us more foolish and never produces good results unless it teaches us at last to get control of ourselves. Greed leads us toward danger even as we think we are moving in a direction that will benefit us. Life is both simpler and more complex than greed tells us. Our inherent Buddha nature is more than capable of revealing everything we need to know. When we allow this nature to express itself, we see that it is relatively easy to know what to do and when to do it. At the same time, we will see that the fullness and perfection of this nature completely transcends anything we can think of.

One of the "tricks" of successful practice of Buddhism is to allow yourself to relax enough so that your inherent Buddha nature can begin to express itself. We can find this ability to relax by upholding the precepts and being satisfied with whatever we have. What more does anyone need than this? If we are upholding the precepts, there is nothing to fear. If we can allow ourselves to relax within our inherent Buddha wisdom, we will see that already we lack nothing. This is the way to find true knowledge of sufficiency. This is the way to be satisfied with whatever you have.

The *Sutra of Bequeathed Teachings* says:

> *Knowing how to be satisfied with whatever one has is the ultimate refuge of peace and security. One who knows how to be satisfied with whatever he has can lie anywhere on the ground and feel completely contented. One who does not know how to be satisfied with what he has will feel that something is lacking even if he is in heaven; one like this is poor even though he may possess enormous wealth. One like this finds only entanglement and suffering in the operation of his senses, while one who knows how to be satisfied finds only comfort and joy in them.*

Good friends are the best of all relatives

"When we are young we must depend on our parents. When we are grown we must depend on our friends."

Parents bear and raise us, but no one can expect to rely on them forever. Eventually we must stand on our own in the company of people we choose to be with. These are our friends: the people we choose to be with. We call them the best of all relatives because friends are people who are drawn to us through karmic bonds that often are much deeper than the familial bonds of this life. Once we learn to appreciate the mysterious attraction that makes people become friends, our capacity for growth in all spheres of life will be very much enhanced. And once we have learned to appreciate our friends, we can begin to learn that all sentient beings are our friends and that all of them deserve our care and consideration at all times.

The *Dirgha Agama* mentions four important aspects of friendship:

1) Stop bad behavior. Good friends tell each other when they see that one of them is doing something wrong. Good friends help each other do the right thing.

2) Be kind. Good friends are happy when they see that their friends are happy and they are sad when they see that their friends are suffering. They praise each other and when they hear others speaking badly of their friends, they correct that person's speech.

3) Help each other. Good friends help each other and do not lead each other into bad practices. If a good friend sees another heading in the wrong direction, he will take him aside and speak to him. He will not correct his friend in front of others.

4) Share the same lot. Good friends do not stint money or goods when their friends are in need. In difficult circumstances, they will even be willing to risk their lives for each other.

The *Fo Shuo Pei Sutra* says that the way to treat friends is "transform evil into good, discuss the Dharma with them often, encourage their best qualities, be kind to them."

The *Dharmagupta Vinaya* says that there are seven things to remember when dealing with friends:

1) Give what is hard to give.

2) Do what is hard to do.

3) Be patient when it is hard to be patient.

4) Do not keep secrets.

5) Protect one another.

6) Do not abandon a friend in time of need.

7) Do not permit an atmosphere of greed or low-mindedness to develop between you.

Good friends support each other. We learn from them and they learn from us. It is important to focus on growth and change among friends. We should accept changes in them and they should accept changes in us. We all should be learning and growing all the time. Among the best friends, change for the better should be welcomed and accepted whenever it occurs.

Once a person becomes a Buddhist, the rest of his life should be dedicated to changing for the better. It is important that our friends accept these changes in us and it is important that we accept and encourage them in our friends. Never allow yourself to be jealous of a friend and never allow yourself to hold them back or prevent them from growing. Their growth is your growth. A friend who is happy and prosperous is a wonderful reflection on you.

> *The bodhisattva,*
> *with his many wise methods,*
> *shines brightly on this saha world.*
> *He leads all sentient beings,*
> *each to understand this truth.*

> —from the *Lotus Sutra*

Nirvana is the Supreme Peace

> *All worlds in all*
> *the ten directions*
> *are a single open eye.*

> — Zen Master Ming Chen

Nirvana is "not born, not dying, not arising, not destroyed." It is the ultimate wisdom and the truth that lies beyond language and beyond all forms of manifest life.

There is suffering in life because all of life is conditioned by four inevitable transformations: coming into being, abiding, being destroyed, emptiness. The very universe in which we live is transformed in exactly this same way. It comes into being, then it abides, then it is destroyed and then it becomes empty. This emptiness is not nothingness. It is a zero point wherein all the potential of the next universe is held in quiet abeyance.

It is important that all of us fully recognize the inevitability of these transformations. Nirvana is beyond them. The peace of the bodhisattva who glimpses Nirvana but stays in this world also fully transcends them.

Nirvana has four basic qualities. These qualities cannot be grasped by the samsaric intellect, but they can be vaguely indicated in words. No description of Nirvana should be clung to, since Nirvana is beyond words.

1) Nothing arises in Nirvana. Nothing arises and nothing dies. Nothing changes in Nirvana. There is no suffering, no trouble, nothing enters and nothing leaves. It is a realm of perfect purity. It is an absolute realm beyond all distinctions, all duality, and all phenomena.

2) Nothing abides in Nirvana. Nothing abides in Nirvana because Nirvana pervades everything and is beyond everything. One who has entered Nirvana is everywhere; (he) is perfect purity, the perfect Dharma, the perfected Tathagata, the fullness of Buddhahood, at one with emptiness.

3) Nirvana is selfless. It is beyond all definition and thus it cannot be said to have any nature or not have any nature. It is selfless and beyond any thought we can have. Whatever you think about Nirvana cannot be the ultimate truth.

4) Nirvana lacks nothing. Nirvana is liberation from all lacking. In Nirvana nothing need be attained.

> Free as the wind and moon,
> the eye within the eye.
> As endless as the universe,
> the light beyond the light.

The shade of the willow,
the brightness of a flower,
the home of everyone.
Knock and you will be let in.

—anonymous Zen poem

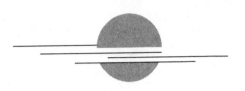

Faith

Because we have faith,
therefore we do no harm.
All merit and all virtue
arise from and are maintained by faith.

— from the *Mahayana Sutralamkara Shastra*

The importance of faith

Faith is the opposite of doubt. Faith causes us to learn the Dharma quickly and penetrate its meaning deeply, because when we have faith we are not hindered at every turn by doubt and suspicion.

The *Avadanas* says, "Faith is that which wants to know the complete truth, that which takes delight in hearing the Dharma, and that which leads to the abandonment of all selfishness."

The *Brahmajala Sutra* says, "All practice stems from faith and all virtue is rooted in it."

The awakening of faith generally establishes the beginning of one's practice of Buddhism. The Fifty-Two Stages of the Bodhi Way described in the *Avatamsaka Sutra* begin with faith. The Five Spiritual Roots and the Five Spiritual Powers of the Thirty-Seven Conditions Leading to Buddhahood also begin with faith. In addition to this, faith is an important theme in almost every Buddhist sutra.

When conditions and karma are right,
the ability to hear the Dharma appears.
And then the practitioner comes under

*the protection of the compassionate vows
of all the Buddhas and bodhisattvas.
And with this, his ability to turn from
suffering is established. In faith
there is Nirvana.*

— from the *Treatise on the Awakening of Faith in the Mahayana*

The *Abhidharmakosha* says that Buddhist practice must be based on a firm belief in the Four Noble Truths, the Triple Gem, and the law of karma.

The *Vijnaptimatratasiddhi Shastra* says:

*What is faith? The essence of faith lies in belief in the
reality of the Buddha's existence, in belief in the virtue of
the Buddha, and in belief in the power of the Buddha. It
also lies in the deep appreciation of the practitioner, in
the joy of the practitioner, in the desire for enlightenment of the practitioner, and in the purity of mind of the
practitioner.*

*Faith cures doubt. Faith inspires one to find delight
in goodness.*

Doubt is one of the eight defilements in the Yogachara school of Buddhism. These eight defilements are unsteadiness, drowsiness, doubt, laziness, shallowness of purpose, poor concentration, a scattered mind, and wrong views. The cure for doubt, as well as all other defilements, is listen to the Dharma, contemplate the Dharma, and practice the Dharma.

*The Dharma is a great ocean which
we enter by faith and cross
by the power of wisdom.*

— from the *Mahaprajnaparamita Shastra*

The *Mahayana Samparigraha Shastra* says that faith is based on three things: 1) The belief that one's inner nature truly is the Buddha nature, 2) The belief that one can attain complete fulfillment within the Buddha nature, and 3) The belief that the Buddha nature holds illimitable virtue and 'merit.

> *The karmic rewards of faith are*
> *the ten wholesome deeds*
> *and revulsion with the sufferings*
> *of birth and death*
> *and desire for supreme enlightenment*
> *and the attainment of Buddhahood.*

— from the *Treatise on the Awakening of Faith in the Mahayana*

The function of faith

Practice without a foundation of faith is difficult and slow at best. Faith helps us to desire goodness as it helps us to raise our level of awareness. Faith is like a light which dispels the darkness of beginningless ignorance and doubt.

The *Avatamsaka Sutra* says:

> *Faith is the source of the way and the mother of all*
> *virtue and merit. It increases all virtue and eradicates*
> *all doubt. It is the beginning of the supreme way.*
>
> *Faith disentangles the mind from the stubbornness*
> *of defilement and destroys the very sources of pride and*
> *arrogance.*
>
> *Faith is the greatest of all treasures. All other*
> *practices depend on the purity of one's faith. Faith can*
> *free the practitioner from all defilement and attachment.*
> *Faith will inspire the practitioner to realize the*
> *marvelous wonders of the deepest truths of the Dharma.*
> *Faith can overcome anything as it establishes all good-*
> *ness. Through faith one ultimately becomes one with the*
> *Tathagata.*
>
> *If the power of one's faith is strong and incorruptible,*
> *then one will achieve purity, clarity and incisiveness.*

*Faith permanently destroys evil and leads to realization
of the untaught truths which lie within us already.
Faith removes obstruction from all Dharma practices.
It disentangles the mind from the eight difficulties and
leads to ease of practice. Faith overcomes all demonic
forces and leads one to the supreme path of liberation.
Faith is the incorruptible seed of all virtue. It nurtures the growth of the bodhi tree. It opens the door of
the highest wisdom and reveals all the Buddhas. For this
reason, faith should be emphasized every step of the way.*

How to increase faith

Faith begins like a sprout in a field. If it receives proper amounts of sun and water, it will grow strong and healthy. If it does not receive the nourishment it needs, then it will wither and die. Just like a sprout in a field, faith is vulnerable and easily harmed. If we associate with the wrong kinds of people or if we constantly subject our awakening minds to the corrosions of doubt, our faith may soon be destroyed. Virtue is sensitive and faith is wise. As we begin to feel the inklings of wisdom and faith we must be careful not to allow ourselves to be overwhelmed by a corresponding increase in sensitivity toward the world around us. There is an old saying that expresses this point well: "When the moral nature rises one foot, the defilements which surround it rise ten feet." Faith, as with all virtue, must be protected and nourished.

Faith can be increased in the following ways:

1) Through the paranormal. Visions of Buddha or the bodhisattvas, paranormal occurrences, and mystical intimations of higher levels of reality are common in Buddhist history. Practitioners should not seek these sorts of experiences, but if one should occur, it should be taken as a stimulant and encouragement to greater faith and greater dedication.

2) Through virtue. Virtue is the finest thing in all of life. Once we begin to understand that all goodness springs from virtue, then our faith will be increased. Our understanding will improve once we

know that true growth can only be attained through study of the Dharma.

3) Through compassion. To understand compassion, we must behave compassionately. Once we have witnessed the effects of compassion and once we have seen the joy it produces, we will understand very deeply that enlightenment is compassion. This understanding gives rise to immense faith in the Dharma.

4) Through wisdom. Wisdom is not the same as intelligence and it has nothing to do with the vanity and cleverness which typify samsaric thinking. In its early stages wisdom manifests as faith; we call it faith because it knows with a power that transcends any reason the mind can give that the Dharma is true and that only it can give rise to complete joy.

5) Through experience. The longer we uphold the precepts of Buddhism, the easier it will be for us to see that the Buddha did not lie. Faith in his teachings can only grow through experience.

6) Through seeing the nature of things. The true nature of all sentient beings is Buddha nature. One glimpse of this truth produces a faith that can never again be shaken.

Faith is especially important when we first begin to practice Buddhism, but the importance of faith does not decrease very much after that. Even though we may be sure of the validity of the Dharma, it is still important for us to rely on faith, for we cannot rise to the next level of realization unless we are sure that that level is there.

Faith to a practitioner is like sun and water to a plant; in the beginning these factors are extremely important and they remain necessary throughout the life of the organism. Faith is that factor that constantly allows us to reach beyond ourselves. Faith shows us again and again that the only path in Buddhism is the path of constant growth.

How to increase the faith of others

The highest form of giving is to give the Dharma. The core of any gift of the Dharma is to give faith in the Dharma to others. Once there is faith, all else will follow. The best way to increase the faith of others is to exhibit it in our own lives. When others see us change for the better due to our practice of Buddhism, their faith in the Dharma will be increased.

When we knowingly attempt to impart the joys of faith to others, we are employing *upaya*, or expedient methods. Since faith is based on a nonverbal tremor within the being, it cannot be transmitted through mundane techniques of persuasion or through rational explanations. Rational explanations may serve as powerful aids in the transmission of faith from one person to another, but in the end it will be our humility, our compassion, and the firm example of our own faith that will have the greatest influence on other people.

While faith can only take root in a person through that person's receptivity, still it must be remembered that the Dharma exists today only because it has been transmitted from one person to another across national borders through centuries of time. We must respect others and allow them to hold their own beliefs, but we should also remember that we ourselves have been blessed with the Dharma only through the labor and compassionate sharing of others.

There is a saying, "Wisdom alone will not lead us to understanding if no one tells us the Dharma."

In the *Mahaparinirvana Sutra*, the Buddha says:

> *If one hundred thousand lamps*
> *are lighted in a single room,*
> *each one will be brilliant*
> *and none will interfere with the others.*
> *The interplay between the self and others*
> *and between me and others is just like this.*

Glossary

alaya-**consciousness** (*alaya-vijnana*; Sanskrit: "storehouse consciousness"): The eighth and most subtle level of consciousness, and the level at which karmic "seeds" are stored.

Amitabha (Sanskrit: "boundless light"): Buddha of mercy and wisdom. Amitabha Buddha is one of the most popular Buddhas in Mahayana Buddhism. He presides over the Western Pure Land.

Ananda (Sanskrit: "bliss"): A principal disciple of the Buddha, he was also the Buddha's cousin. He is famous for his excellent memory and for his humility and devotion.

anuttara samyak sambhodi (Sanskrit: "unexcelled complete enlightenment"): Complete, unexcelled enlightenment, an attribute of all Buddhas.

arhat (Sanskrit: "worthy one"): One who has attained the highest level of Buddhist learning. See Four Fruits.

arupadhatu: See Three Realms.

Avalokiteshvara (Sanskrit: "he who contemplates the sounds of the world"): One of the great bodhisattvas of Mahayana Buddhism. Avalokiteshvara Bodhisattva can manifest in any conceivable form to bring help wherever it is needed. In China, Avalokiteshvara is usually portrayed in female form. In this form, she is called Kuan Yin.

bodhi (Sanskrit: "enlightenment"): Enlightenment. Awakening to one's own Buddha nature.

bodhi mind (*bodhichitta*; Sanskrit: "enlightenment mind"): The enlightened mind or the mind that seeks enlightenment.

bodhi way: The way to enlightenment. The path of a Buddhist who is actively seeking enlightenment.

bodhisattva (Sanskrit: "enlightened being"): (1) Any person who is seeking Buddhahood. (2) A "saint" who stands right on the edge of Nirvana, but remains in this world to help others achieve enlightenment.

bodhisattva vow: The fundamental vow of a bodhisattva to save all sentient beings from delusion and suffering.

Buddha (Sanskrit: "awakened one"): There are innumerable Buddhas in the universe. Shakyamuni Buddha was the "historical" Buddha who taught the Dharma on earth. He is generally thought to have lived between 463–383 BCE.

Buddha nature: The inherent nature that exists in all beings. In Mahayana Buddhism, enlightenment is a process of uncovering this inherent nature.

conditions The present matrix of phenomena. "Conditioned arising" or "conditioned genesis" means all phenomena arise out of other phenomena and none of them has a nature of its own. "Dependent origination" is a synonym for "conditioned arising."

Confucius (Chinese: K'ung Tzu; 551–479 BCE) An early Chinese moral philosopher. Confucianism, the philosophy named after Confucius, was the official philosophy of China between the third century BCE and the fall of the Ch'ing Dynasty in 1911.

Dharma (Sanskrit; "carrying, holding"): The teachings of the Buddha, which carry or hold the truth.

Dharmakaya (Sanskrit: "body of the Dharma, body of the great order"): The Buddha nature identical with transcendental reality.

The unity of the Buddha with everything that exists. One of the three Buddha bodies (*trikaya*), the other two being the Sambhogakaya and the Nirmanakaya.

Eight Sufferings Sakyamuni Buddha said that there are eight basic sufferings in life: birth, age, sickness, death, parting with what we love, meeting with what we don't like, unmet needs, and the ills of the Five Skandhas.

Eight Winds: Profit and loss, defamation and fame, praise and blame, suffering and joy. Shakyamuni Buddha taught that these eight conditions, or "winds," are a natural part of life.

Eightfold Path: See Noble Eightfold Path.

empty, emptiness (Sanskrit: *shunyata*): Having no essence or permanent aspect whatsoever. All phenomena are empty. Sometimes translated as "transparent" or "open."

Fifty-Two Stages of the Bodhi Way: A detailed analysis, presented in the *Avatamsaka Sutra*, of the stages leading from ordinary consciousness to the complete enlightenment of a Buddha.

Five Precepts: The five basic moral precepts of Buddhism: no killing, no stealing, no lying, no sexual misconduct, no use of drugs or alcohol.

Four Fruits: Four stages of spiritual attainment in the Theravadan tradition: "stream-winner" (*shrotapanna*), "once-returner" (*sakadagami*), "never-returner" (*anagami*), "foe-destroyer" (*arhat*).

Four Immeasurable States of Mind (Sanskrit: *chatvari-apramanani*): Four boundless aspects of the Buddha mind: boundless kindness (*maitri*), boundless compassion (*karuna*), boundless joy (*mudita*), boundless equanimity (*upeksa*).

Four Noble Truths : The basic truths of Buddhism: (1) the truth of suffering (*duhkha*), (2) the truth of the origin of suffering (*samudaya*), 3) the truth of the cessation of suffering (*nirodha*), 4) the truth of the path that leads to the cessation of suffering (*marga*).

Four Vows: The four universal vows of a Buddha or bodhisattva. They are: 1) to save all beings without limit, 2) to end all passions and delusions, 3) to learn all methods for doing this, 4) to become perfect in the Dharma.

Hell: The lowest realm of conscious existence. The lowest of the Six Realms. There are many Hell realms. In all of them suffering is so intense that little or no progress can be made toward enlightenment.

Hsing Sze (?–740): An important disciple of Hui Neng. Master Hsing Sze was instrumental in establishing Zen as a major branch of Chinese Buddhism.

Hungry Ghosts: The second lowest of the Six Realms of existence. If hungry ghosts eat or drink, the food turns into fire in their throats.

Hsuan Tsang (600–664): One of China's four great translators of Buddhist sutras. Hsuan Tsang is famous for having traveled to India to obtain Buddhist sutras. He was one of the founders of the Fa Hsiang School, the Chinese form of Yogachara.

Fan Chung-yen (989–1052): A Sung Dynasty government official who grew up in a Buddhist monastery. Fan was a great benefactor to Buddhism.

Hui Neng (638–713): Sixth Patriarch, or leader, of Chinese Zen (Ch'an) Buddhism.

Hui Yuan (334–416): A student of Tao An and the first patriarch of Pure Land Buddhism in China.

kalpa (Sanskrit: "world cycle, world age"): An extremely long period of time; an eon.

kamadhatu: See Three Realms.

karma (Sanskrit: "work, action"): The universal law of cause and effect. All intentional deeds produce effects. The effects of a deed may be experienced instantly or they may not be felt until after many years, or even many lifetimes.

Kshitigarbha (Sanskrit: "womb of the earth"): One of the great bodhisattvas of Mahayana Buddhism. Kshitigarbha Bodhisattva has vowed to remain in Hell until all sentient beings have been released from it.

Kumarajiva (344–413): Born in Kucha, Central Asia. One of China's four great translators of Buddhist sutras. Kumarajiva's translations are remarkable for their fluidity and are still popular today.

Mahasthamaprapta: One of the principal bodhisattvas in Amitabha Buddha's Western Pure Land; subject of one of the chapters of the *Shurangama Sutra*.

Mahayana: One of the two great branches of Buddhism (Theravada being the other). Mahayana Buddhism stresses compassion above asceticism.

Maitreya (Sanskrit: "loving one"): Maitreya is the Buddha of the future. He will be the fifth, and last, earthly Buddha.

Manjushri (Sanskrit: "noble and gentle one"): The bodhisattva of wisdom.

Medicine Buddha (Sanskrit: Bhaisajyaguru): The Buddha of healing. He presides over the Eastern Pure Land.

Nirvana (Sanskrit: "extinction"): Extinction of all causes leading to rebirth. The ultimate goal of all Buddhist practice. Nirvana is not complete annihilation, but rather another mode of existence.

Noble Eightfold Path: The path leading to enlightenment, taught by Shakyamuni Buddha. It is comprised of right view, right thought, right speech, right action, right livelihood, right effort, right mindfulness, and right concentration.

Paramita (Sanskrit: "that which has reached the other shore"): Transcendental truth. See Six Paramitas.

Parinirvana: The Great Nirvana of Shakyamuni Buddha. His death.

prajna (Sanskrit: "consciousness, wisdom"): The highest wisdom. Insight into the emptiness of all phenomena.

pratyeka-buddha (Sanskrit: "solitary awakened one"): One who attains enlightenment on his own, without having heard the teachings of a Buddha.

Pure Land: A Buddha realm. In Mahayana Buddhism, there are countless Buddhas and countless Buddha realms.

rupadhatu: See Three Realms.

Ryokan (1758–1831): A great Japanese monk of the Soto sect of Zen Buddhism, famous for his beautiful poetry.

saha **world** (Sanskrit: *saha-lokadhatu,* "enduring-world"): This world of delusion, the world in which Shakyamuni Buddha preached.

Shakyamuni (Sanskrit: "Sage of the Shakyas"; given name Siddhartha Gautama): The historical Buddha; founder of Buddhism. He is generally thought to have lived between 463–383 BCE.

samadhi (Sanskrit: "establish, make firm"): A very high level of meditative concentration.

Samantabhadra (Sanskrit: "he who is all-pervadingly good"): One of the great bodhisattvas of Mahayana Buddhism; one of the four most revered bodhisattvas of Chinese tradition.

samsara (Sanskrit: "journeying"): Delusion. Deluded mental formations that keep the mind trapped in the cycle of birth and death.

Sangha (Sanskrit: "crowd"): The Buddhist community. All followers of Buddhism. In Chinese, Sangha usually refers only to Buddhist monks and nuns.

Shariputra: One of the principal disciples of Shakyamuni Buddha, remembered for his wisdom and learning.

Siddhanta (Sanskrit: "doctrinal view"): In the *Mahaprajnaparamita Shastra*, the Four Siddhanta are the four levels of the Buddha's teachings.

Six Paramitas: The six "perfections" or virtues practiced by an enlightened being: generosity, upholding the precepts, patience, energetic progress, meditation, and wisdom.

Six Realms: The various modes of existence in which rebirth occurs, ranging from the lower realms of hell, hungry ghosts, and animals to the higher realms of humans, titans, and gods.

six senses: The five senses of sight, smell, hearing, taste, and touch, plus the cognitive processes that coordinate them.

Sixth Patriarch: see Hui Neng

skandha (Sanskrit: "aggregate, heap"): The five *skandha* that make up a human being are: form, feeling, perception, mental formation, and consciousness.

shravaka (Sanskrit: "one who heard"): Any one of the Buddha's personal disciples.

Su Tung-p'o (1036–1101): One of China's greatest poets, he was also a devout Buddhist.

sutra (Sanskrit: 'threads'): That which is "threaded together," by extension, the sacred scriptures of Buddhism.

T'ai Hsu (1899–1947): A modern Chinese Buddhism reformer, and the first proponent of a modern humanistic Buddhism.

Mount T'ai: A famous mountain located in Shandong Province.

T'ang dynasty (618–905): Until the imperial suppression of Buddhism in 845, the T'ang dynasty was China's greatest period of Buddhism.

Tao An (312-385): One of China's greatest Buddhist preachers, famous for his ability to speak about the Dharma.

Tathagata (Sanskrit: "thus come one"): One of the ten titles of the Buddha.

Tathagatagarbha (Sanskrit: "womb of the Tathagata"): That which holds the Tathagata within itself; i.e. all sentient beings. A near synonym for "Buddha nature."

Ten Wholesome Deeds: No killing, no stealing, no sexual misconduct, no lying, no duplicity, no harsh words, no flattery, no greed, no anger, no ignorance.

Theravada: One of the two great branches of Buddhism (Mahayana is the other one). Theravada Buddhism stresses individual enlightenment above all else.

Thirty-Seven Conditions Leading to Buddhahood: The thirty-seven basic conditions conducive to enlightenment. See the *Agamas* for more detail.

Three Dharma Seals: The three basic characteristics of existence. They are: 1) impermanence; 2) the interconnectedness of all things, and thus the absence of a self or essence in anything; and 3) Nirvana.

Three Poisons: Greed, anger, and ignorance. The sources of all delusion and suffering in this world.

Three Realms (Sanskrit: *triloka*): Three different realms that make up *samsara*. The cycle of the existence of all beings in the Six Realms takes place within the Three Realms. The Three Realms are: the realm of desire (*kamadhatu*), the realm of form (*rupadhatu*) and the realm of formlessness (*arupadhatu*).

Triple Gem: Buddha, Dharma, and Sangha (the Buddha, his teaching, and the community of Buddhists).

trividya (Sanskrit: "three insights"): The three insights that all phenomena are impermanent, sorrowful, and devoid of essence.

Twelve Nidanas(Sanskrit: "links"): The twelve links in the chain of conditioned arising. They are: ignorance, impulse, consciousness, name and form, the six senses, contact, sensation, craving, clinging, existence, birth, death.

upaya (Sanskrit: "skillful means"): The methods and skills used by a Buddha or bodhisattva to guide others toward enlightenment.

Yin Kuang (1862–1940): Thirteenth patriarch of Chinese Pure Land Buddhism.

Yogachara (Sanskrit: "application of yoga"): A form of Mahayana Buddhism whose central notion is that everything knowable can only be known through the mind, and thus, everything is "mind only."

Zen (Sanskrit: *dhyana*, "meditation"; Chinese: Ch'an): One of the most important of the eight schools of Chinese Buddhism. Zen Buddhism generally emphasizes enlightenment over ritual practice.

Sutras Cited in the Text

The sutras mentioned in the text are listed here in alphabetical order, followed by their titles in the Chinese Buddhist canon.

Abhidharma Samgiti Paryayapada (A Pi Ta Mo Chi Yi Men Tsu Lun)

Abhidharmakosha (Chü She Lun)

Abhiniskramana Sutra (Fo Pen Hsing Chi Ching)

Adbhutadharma Sutra (Fo Shuo Wei Ts'eng Yu Yin Yüan Ching)

Avadanas (Ch'u Yao Ching)

Avatamsaka Sutra (Ta Fang Kuang Fo Hua Yen Ching)

Bodhisattva Gocharopaya Visaya Vikurvana Nirdesha Sutra (Sa Che Ni Chien Tzu Ching)

Bodhisattva Without Possessions Sutra (P'u Sa Wu Suo Yu Ching)

Bodhisattvabhumi Shastra (P'u Sa Ti Ch'ih Lun)

Brahmajala Sutra (Fan Wang Ching)

Buddha's Medicine Sutra (Fo Yi Ching)

Chu Fa Chi Yao Sutra (Chu Fa Chi Yao Ching)

Collection of Dharmas Sutra (Fa Chi Ching)

Contemplations on the Basis of Mind Sutra (Ta Ch'eng Pen Sheng Hsin Ti Kuan Ching)

Control of the Body Sutra (Fo Chih Shen Ching)

Dharmagupta Vinaya (Szu Fen Lü)

Dharmapada (Fa Chü Ching)

Dharmapadavadana Sutra (Fa Chü P'i Yü Ching)

Diamond Sutra (Vajracchedika Prajnaparamita Sutra; Chin Kang Ching)

Dirgha Agama (Ch'ang Ah Han Ching)

Eight Realizations of the Bodhisattva Sutra (Pa Ta Jen Chüeh Ching)

Ekottarika Agama (Tseng Yi Ah Han Ching)

Fayuan Chulin (Fa Yüan Chu Lin)

Five-Part Vinaya (Wu Fen Lü)

Fo Shuo Pei Sutra (Fo Shuo Pei Ching)

Great Collection of True Dharmas Sutra (Ta Chi Hui Cheng Fa Ching)

Instructions Pertaining to the Royal Samadhi of Contemplating the Buddha (Pao Wang San Mei Nien Fo Chih Chih)

Introduction to the Stages of the Dharma Realm (Fa Chieh Ts'e Ti Ch'u Men)

Jataka Nidana (Fo Shuo Sheng Ching)

Karmavibhanga Sutra (Yeh Pao Ch'a Pieh Ching)

Kushalamula Samgraha Sutra (Hua Shou Ching)

Lankavatara Sutra (Leng Ch'ieh Ching)

Lotus Sutra (Saddharmapundarika Sutra; Fa Hua Ching)

Lung Shu's Expanded Treatise on the Pure Land (Lung Shu Tseng Kuang Ching T'u Wen)

Magnificent Life of the Prince Sutra (T'ai Tzu Jui Ying Pen Ch'i Ching)

Mahaparinirvana Sutra (Ta Po Nieh P'an Ching)

Mahaprajnaparamita Shastra (Ta Chih Tu Lun)

Mahaprajnaparamita Sutra (Ta Po Jo P'o Luo Mi Tuo Ching)

Maharatnakuta (Ta Pao Chi Ching)

Mahasamnipata (Ta Chi Ching)

Mahasanghika Vinaya (Mo Ho Seng Ch'i Lü)

Mahayana Samparigraha Shastra (She Ta Ch'eng Lun)

Mahayana Sutralamkara Shastra (Ta Chuang Yen Ching Lun)

Meditation on the Three Contemplations Sutra (Tsuo Ch'an San Kuan Ching)

Parinirvana Sutra: Fo Po Ni Huan Ching

Patience of Rahula Sutra (Luo Yün Jen Ju Ching)

Platform Sutra of the Sixth Patriarch (Liu Tsu T'an Ching)

Questions of the Precious Girl Sutra (Pao Nü Suo Wen Ching)

Rain of Treasures Sutra (Pao Yü Ching)

Saddharma Smriti Upasthana Sutra (Cheng Fa Nien Ch'u Ching)

Samantabhadrotsahana Parivarta Sutra (Kuan P'u Hsien P'u Sa Hsing Fa Ching)

Samyukta Agama (Tsa Ah Han Ching)

Satyasiddhi Shastra (Ch'eng Shih Lun)

Shurangama Sutra (Leng Yen Ching)

Sigalovada Sutra (Shan Sheng Ching)

Six Paramitas Sutra (Liu P'o Luo Mi Ching)

Sukhavativyuha Sutra (Wu Liang Shou Ching)

Suratapariprccha Sutra (Hsü Lai Ching)

Sutra Concerning Four Kinds of Self-Harming (Szu Tzu Ch'in Ching)

Sutra in Forty-Two Sections (Szu Shih Erh Chang Ching)

Sutra of Bequeathed Teachings (Fo Yi Chiao Ching)

Sutra of One Hundred Parables (Pai Yü Ching)

Sutra on Distinguishing Between the Origins of Good and Evil (Fen Pieh Shan E Suo Ch'i Ching)

Sutra on the Compassionate Upaya of the Buddha (Ta Fang Pien Fo Pao En Ching)

Sutra on the Principles of the Six Paramitas (Ta Ch'eng Li Ch'ü Liu P'o Luo Mi Ching)

Treatise on the Awakening of Faith in the Mahayana (Ta Ch'eng Ch'i Hsin Lun)

T'sai Ken T'an

Upasakashila Sutra (Yu P'o Se Chieh Ching)

Vijnaptimatratasiddhi Shastra (Ch'eng Wei Shih Lun)

Vimalakirti Nirdesha Sutra (Wei Mo Ching)

Yogacharabhumi Shastra (Yü Ch'ieh Shih Ti Lun)

Yogacharabhumi Sutra (Hsiu Hsing Tao Ti Ching)

About the Author

MASTER HSING YUN was ordained at the age of fifteen at Chi Xia Shan Monastery in Jiangsu, China. He has spent well over fifty years teaching the Dharma. He is the founder both of Fo Guang Shan monastery in Taiwan and of the Buddha's Light International Association, a world-wide organization dedicated to the propagation of Buddhism. Master Hsing Yun is the forty-eighth patriarch in the Linchi School of Zen Buddhism, and author of numerous books and essays on Buddhism.

The "weathermark" identifies this book as a production of Weatherhill, Inc., publishers of fine books on Asia and the Pacific. Editorial supervision, book and cover design: David S. Noble. Production supervision: Bill Rose. Printing and binding: R.R. Donnelley & Sons. The typeface used is Fairfield, with Stone Informal for display.